D1556145

Arthur Billitt

The Joy of Gardening

Ward Lock Limited·London

Acknowledgements

The publishers gratefully acknowledge Bob Challinor, who took all the black-and-white and colour photographs.

All line drawings are by Gay Galsworthy. The publishers also gratefully acknowledge Auriol (Guildford) Ltd (Fig. 2), Wolf Tools Ltd (Fig. 8a) and Spear & Jackson (Tools) Ltd (Fig. 8b & c) for their help in providing illustrative material from which these drawings were made. Figs. 16 and 19a are after *The Fruit Garden Displayed*, pp. 59–60 and 25 respectively, published by the Royal Horticultural Society, 1978. Fig. 20 is after the line drawing on pp. 11 in *Percy Thrower's Guide to Gardeners' World*, BBC/Hamlyn, 1973.

First published in Great Britain in 1983 by Ward Lock Limited, 82 Gower Street, London WC1E 6EQ, a Pentos Company.

House editor Denis Ingram
Text filmset in Monophoto Plantin Light 11 on 13 pt by Santype International Ltd., Salisbury, Wilts.

Printed and bound in Italy by Sagdos SpA.

British Library Cataloguing in Publication Data

Billitt, Arthur
   The joy of gardening
   1. Gardening
   I. Title
   635   SB450.97

ISBN 0-7063-6238-1

Contents

Preface

The secrets of successful gardening unfold with experience for which I believe there is no substitute. To get the best results from your own garden, the sublime happiness and the satisfaction of doing the job yourself, or better still with your partner, it is necessary to do the right things at the right time in the right way.

I was privileged to have been born in Cambridgeshire where horticultural expertise was always close at hand. Sole possession of a small plot in my parents' garden at the age of six started my lifelong interest in gardening. Subsequent house moves took me to Evesham with its very heavy clay soil and to Nottingham with its contrasting light bunter sand.

At this time I was engaged in the development of Lenton Research Station. Here the soil was very varied – everything from poor sandy gravel to red Nottingham marl. Subsequently I undertook the task of cultivating 45 acres of ill-drained, ultra-heavy clay at Thurgarton, which ultimately became the home of a successful fruit growing research unit.

Since those days with the Boots Company, 27 years of endeavour at Clack's Farm has transformed $2\frac{1}{2}$ acres within a derelict property into a garden well known to viewers of BBC 2 'Gardeners' World' programmes and visited during the last 12 years by over a quarter of a million gardeners from all over the country. Prior to the quest for Clack's Farm it had always been a case of finding the house first and then finding out something about the soil and endeavouring to make the best of it. It was experience with soils that convinced me in 1954 that I should go armed with a spade wherever I went to look for property; the need to alter a house did not deter me but changing the nature of a soil is much more difficult, in fact often impossible. In the case of Clack's Farm, the house was in a terrible condition but the soil, although exhausted, clearly had potential.

Nothing succeeds like success and gardening is no exception. I do hope that what I have written from a lifetime's experience will help you, the reader, not only to be a successful gardener but to enjoy it as much as Riet and I do at Clack's Farm, for to us it is great fun. With best wishes for successful and happy gardening.

A.W.B.

ONE

Managing the soil and compost making

Cultivating the soil

Soil types vary considerably, from the heaviest clay to light blow-away sand and so much depends on the way in which they are individually handled. After years of experience with several different types of clay soil I have come to the conclusion that the only practical answer for all heavy soils is winter digging followed by surface cultivations in the spring. I have a hard and fast rule which involves the use of a full sized spade to ensure that the depth of the digging is right; a near worn out spade does not turn the soil over deep enough. Another point: each spadeful must be completely turned over and the clods left intact, I do not slice them with the spade. Our winter frosts usually start soon after Christmas which is the reason why all my digging is done before that time, there is nothing like a thorough freezing for breaking up a heavy soil, it is the freezing of the water within that does the trick. In addition, winter rains and winds contribute to the taming process which goes on slowly but continuously until the spring.

The secret is to keep off the roughly dug soil until the spring and on no account re-dig it either early in the spring or during the growing season. The time for action is March when the winds start to blow, then before the clods have time to dry out I am out with a Wolf three-pronged cultivator to break them down. Tackled this way it is neither difficult nor exhausting as the lumps of soil instead of being solid are crumbly. With this first surface cultivation completed it is soon time, usually a couple of days later, for a second run through with the cultivator. After that it is just a question of whether the ground is needed for a seed-bed or for planting. For a seed-bed I bring out a rake which is still the best tool for getting a fine tilth which is so essential for small seeds. The question of whether lime should be used in an attempt to improve a clay soil depends on several factors, the pH for instance may already be high enough in which case the addition of lime could create other problems. However, if the pH is relatively low and the plants to be grown are not lime haters, liming would be an advantage. Garden lime is best applied during the winter at a time when the clods are frozen hard. Incidentally I have used some of the products claimed to improve clay soils but none justified the cost involved.

It is the winter digging that keeps both the soil and the gardener fit. Note the depth of each spadeful turned over and the roughness of the dug surface.

Action (early March) with the Wolf three-pronged cultivator, breaking down the clods. Stage one in preparing a seed-bed.

The easiest soils to manage are those that fall between the two extremes, medium loams which are mixtures of clay and sand but again the winter digging and surface-cultivations routine produce the best results. Whilst most of the heavy and medium soils have reasonably good natural levels of fertility when they are properly handled, the light sands or gravelly soils are usually poor and need boosting with liberal amounts of organic matter to hold the moisture and to supply the plant nutrients is a constant problem – hence the advice to dig and cultivate them in the spring rather than before Christmas.

For the maintenance of fertility in all types of cultivated soil it is necessary to return in some form bulky organic matter to compensate for the continuous breakdown and loss processes. These natural processes go on at a much greater rate in light sandy and gravelly soils than in the medium loams or heavy clays, which means that whilst the addition of compost or manure is necessary for the maintenance of fertility, on light soils the quantity needed is much greater than on the heavier soils. However, the wise gardener will always conserve all garden waste material except woody stuff and those weeds in the process of producing seed. No compost in the making produces enough heat to kill any weed seed.

Compost making

It is this waste, including autumn leaves and lawn mowings, that should go back into the soil in the form of well-rotted compost. By incorporating decaying compost into the soil food is provided for the soil bacteria and fungi; they in turn play their part in the process which results in the release of natural plant nutrients. There is nothing magic about compost making but it does take time to do the job properly, in fact I work on a 12 months' basis, clearing the bins of finished friable compost in October and starting afresh with autumn leaves immediately afterwards. (Any incompletely decomposed vegetation is kept back for incorporation with the new 'starting' material – see below.) I have never attempted to make quick compost as I believe that it is best to stay as close to nature as possible.

Over the years I have made compost in open heaps, which is messy because the birds scratch it about looking for worms and insects. Now we have two slatted wooden bins 5 × 5 × 5 ft (1.5 × 1.5 × 1.5 m) which work well and enable us to make large quantities of the finest finished product (Fig. 1). The front slats fit into slots and lift out for easy filling and emptying. We always start our bins with a 7 in (18 cm) layer of green material laid directly on the soil, which allows the worms access to play their part in the decaying processes. As with

Fig. 1 Construction of Clack's Farm compost bins.
Each bin is constructed from 4in (10 cm) square softwood posts, previously treated
in horticultural wood preservative, on to which are nailed, on three sides, the $\frac{3}{4}$ in
(2 cm) thick side panels. The posts are sunk 2 ft (60 cm) into the ground. Note that
the front panels slide in a slot and are removable and that ventilation is ensured by
keeping the panels apart by means of small chocks of wood.

subsequent layers this one is trampled down a little especially round the edges, before sprinkling a handful of garden lime over it. Then when the next 7 in (18 cm) layer is complete and consolidated it gets a sprinkling of our own garden soil. This alternate layer treatment goes on until the bin is full, which takes a long time as the slow but sure rotting processes result in a continuous shrinkage of the bulk. The garden lime keeps the contents of the bins sweet providing it has not been made with too much lawn mowings. The garden soil introduces soil bacteria and fungi which multiply rapidly; their contribution to good compost making is most important.

This system does not work when lawn mowings are the main source of starting material. We have overcome the problem by treating each layer of grass mowings with PBI Recycler and instead of finishing up with a revolting sticky mess, we have been able to make a very acceptable friable compost from lawn mowings only.

Each October we always have some partially rotted compost on the top of each bin, this we use for the fresh start; it would be a mistake to add it to the land in that condition. Again, it is a question of making the best use of the soil bacteria – if they were confronted with this unrotted vegetation they would take up the nitrogen from the soil to assist them in breaking the vegetation down. Then plants growing in the soil might well suffer from a nitrogen deficiency. Of course there

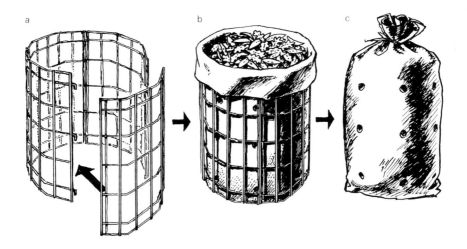

Fig. 2 Construction of Auriol composter.
(*a*) The empty and complete wire frame comprising four frame sections, showing how the sections are linked together by connecting hooks. (*b*) With plastic liner inserted and bin full of compost. (*c*) Plastic liner tied at top and wire frame removed so that another 'bin' can be started.

are ways and means of correcting the deficiency but it would mean applying extra amounts of nitrogenous fertilizers.

In addition we make compost successfully in wire netting circles. For this we use 2 in (5 cm) mesh, 4 ft (1.2 m) wide chicken wire netting; this is supported by four to six wooden or metal stakes. Our other compost bin, made by Auriol, comprises a simple, firm metal wire frame holding a bottomless plastic bag; when the bag is filled we lift the frame away, place the frame in a new location, insert a new plastic bag and we are then ready to start the filling process again (Fig. 2). Incidentally there are air holes in the sides of the plastic bags.

It is this understanding of the basic soil fertility principles that has enabled us to bring Clack's Farm garden back to a high level of fertility, an essential ingredient for successful gardening.

TWO

The joys of gardening under cover

Greenhouses

My love of plants is such that I want to be with them every day. From April to September that is no problem, there is much to be done outside and the garden is alive with plant growth activity. However, when autumn sets in with its shorter hours of daylight and lower temperatures plants outside in the garden settle down for their winter rest. It is at this time that we have at least one greenhouse full of colour and what a joy it is to be inside gardening happily, especially when it is cold and raining outside.

A greenhouse with sufficient heating to maintain a minimum temperature of 45°F (7°C) is our aim: in a 20 × 10 ft (3 × 6 m) Alton cedar wood house, a 10 ft (3 m) Heatmor paraffin/water heater with a double bank of hot water pipes has proved very economical and efficient. The blue flame burner, with no poisonous fumes to cause even a smell, ensures plant safety. To make sure that on a very cold night the temperature does not drop below 45°F (7°C) we have a Humex electric fan heater at the ready with its thermostat pre-set. At a relatively low cost this cuts out all the worries about chilled plants or even frozen ones. Of course 45°F (7°C) is too low a temperature for germinating seeds, quite a lot of them needing 60–70°F (15–21°C) for quick and satisfactory germination.

For my Christmas Day sowing of onions and a week or two later the begonias etc. we use a couple of propagating frames, one a Big Top made by Humex, the other a home-made wooden one heated by a Humex soil heating cable. Both function extremely well, the thermostats being sensitive enough to respond to a single-degree change in temperature. In both propagators the heating cables warm the sand base and the air. In addition to these largish propagators we have two Ward propagators in which the heating elements are enclosed completely for safety; they have built-in thermostats pre-set at 62°F (17°C), a temperature high enough for germinating most seeds. These propagators have given us almost as good results as the more elaborate and more costly ones. We find the cost of running a propagator low, due to the limited space heated, but the benefits and pleasures are great, giving us the pleasure of growing all our own plants from seed.

Every packet of seed I sow gives me a thrill as once again I realize that I am participating in nature's realm of living miracles.

Apart from anything else I find that by growing my own plants, sowing them at the right time (Fig. 3), pricking them out at the right stage, hardening off and planting out before they get root-bound, I am able to grow plants that are healthy, happy and look it from the seedling stage onwards. It is this involvement with plants that makes gardening such an absorbing hobby and by growing your own you get full value and many bonuses for your contribution. Another point, starting with packets of seed means that you have a far greater choice of varieties; for instance, commercially grown bedding plants are usually run-of-the-mill varieties which compare badly with the vastly superior, more recently introduced varieties which are now freely available to the gardener.

I have mentioned 'hardening off' – this is a gradual process of getting greenhouse-raised plants acclimatized to the outside lower temperatures, and can be done more satisfactorily with home-raised plants. The problem with most commercially grown plants is that they are often grown quickly, far too crowded and in too high a temperature, a combination which usually results in weak, drawn plants.

It is not absolutely necessary to have a heated greenhouse but without heat in a greenhouse sowing dates will have to be later and the range of plants that can be grown from seed will be limited. Nevertheless the possibilities with a cold greenhouse are considerable. For instance when I lived in Nottingham I always planted my tomatoes out in a cold greenhouse round about the third week in April; sometimes they went blue but none failed to recover and crop well. Now at Clack's Farm we have great fun growing melons, grapes, cucumbers and tomatoes in greenhouses without heat.

Whether a greenhouse is heated or not, automatic ventilators are a great boon – gone are the days when it was necessary to rush out to open up every time the sun came out. Without ventilation it does not need much sun-heat to raise greenhouse temperatures in a few minutes to over $100°F$ ($38°C$) and then the plants can be in for a real roasting.

Not all plants enjoy full sunshine, for example *Achimenes,* gloxinias, *Streptocarpus,* to name but a few, are much happier when we cover their side of the greenhouse with shading to break the direct sunlight.

I have long favoured wooden-framed greenhouses; the climate inside always has had the better growing feel about it. Now after having had the opportunity of carrying out a 12-month research project comparing the pros and cons of wood versus metal I am more than convinced that on all counts wood is the better buy. Metal with its

Fig. 3   Sowing seed in a seed tray.
(*a*) Slightly overfill tray with seed compost and tap tray to settle the compost.
(*b*) Remove excess mix with a straight edge. (*c*) Firm gently with a rectangular
presser-board. (*d*) Sow seeds thinly and as evenly as possible. (*e*) Cover the seeds
with sieved seed compost. (*f*) Place a sheet of glass covered with newspaper over
tray: remove both on germination of seeds.

a   F₁ hybrid geraniums grown from seed. (**a**) Note the care taken in handling each   b
seedling. (**b**) Seedling being potted in a 4 in (10 cm) pot. Note that the fingers
only are used for firming the peat-based potting compost.

higher heat/cold conductivity costs appreciably more to heat, especially in very cold weather; on warm or hot days the air is drier and more watering is needed than in the wooden-framed house. In addition, according to our observations red spider mite is a greater problem in the metal-framed greenhouses.

When asked to advise on the size of a greenhouse I always suggest that it should be larger than the would-be buyer has in mind, once you start greenhouse gardening it is never large enough. Apart from limited growing space, very small greenhouses are difficult to keep cool in summer. I would recommend nothing smaller than 10 × 8 ft or 12 × 10 ft (3 × 2.4 m or 3.6 × 3 m). In buying a greenhouse you make an investment in gardening happiness, make sure that it is well constructed then it will last for years. I have yet to meet the gardener who has been satisfied with the cheap flimsy, plastic versions of the real thing; take my advice and start with a good greenhouse, a false start can be expensive and disappointing.

Cold frames

Whilst unheated cold frames with Dutch lights are less popular now, no doubt due to the cost of the timber, possession of one can be a valuable asset. During the winter ours is usually full of lettuce, then in April it is in use for hardening off bedding plants, by the end of May 'Sweetheart' melons go into it; it is never empty for more than a few days. Even during the severe weather in the winter of 1981/1982, when temperatures fell to −24°C, 'Arctic King' lettuces overwintered well in our cold frame. The plants were not watered again after planting, good ventilation preventing mildew becoming a problem.

Cloches

Each spring we defeat the chilling effects of our weather by covering rows of lettuce, peas, broad beans, early potatoes, radishes, etc. with cloches, the simple protection they provide allowing us to get the crops ready at least a month earlier. My preference is for glass-covered cloches; contrary to general belief the risk of frost damage to plants under plastic-covered cloches is far greater than with no covering at all. In common with growing plants in greenhouses and cold frames, ventilation for those under cloches is also needed, so ours are always placed with an inch or two (2.5–5 cm) gap between each one in the row. We use Westray cloches – they have the added advantage of netting under the glass so that at times the cloches without the glass can be used to protect rows of crops against the birds.

Greenhouse tomatoes, melons and cucumbers

Now a word about greenhouse tomatoes which I really do enjoy growing. There are few, if any, plants more responsive to treatment

Overwintered 'Arctic King' lettuce in a cold frame, being stimulated into growth by breaking the soil surface with a small cultivator.

whether it be good or bad, than tomatoes, that is why they are so extensively used in research for work on plant nutrition and for the checking of possible phytotoxicity (plant tissue poison) of insecticides and fungicides. Whilst heating a whole greenhouse for our tomatoes is too expensive I have found that by germinating the seed in a propagating frame early in March, I can manage the rest of the way by growing the plants cool; in fact the end results have proved better than when we kept the young plants at 60°F (15°C). One thing I have noticed is that our tomato seedlings grown on slowly at 50°F (10°C) during the day and 45°F (7°C) at night do not now go blue when they are planted out towards the end of April in a cold greenhouse.

For the last few years I have switched over from planting in the border to grow-bags and have had no difficulty in justifying the extra cost. Even in the shortened, without-heat growing season two 'Alicante' plants per bag have never failed to crop less than 20 lb (9 kg) of ripe fruit per plant. The secret of success here is that we spray the bottom trusses of flowers with Betapal (a tomato fruit setting spray) to make sure that we get a complete set, then when the tomatoes show signs of swelling we start our routine weekly feeding with a high potash liquid fertilizer. It is the high potash that keeps the plants healthy, ensures quality and quick ripening fruit. To keep the plants free from disease it is important to ventilate well, particularly in damp weather, to encourage air circulation around the plants. I remove the lower foliage when the ripening fruit above it has changed colour. In very hot or very damp weather an electric fan to circulate the air is of great benefit.

I also get a lot of pleasure out of growing melons in a small 12 × 8 ft (3.6 × 2.4 m) greenhouse, again without heat. We have fixed up a metal framework which slopes inwards, which means that the melon plants also hang inwards; this makes training and hand pollination of the female flowers easy. Since going back to growing on raised mounds of old turf the plants have done better and do not get a tired look as the growing season progresses. 'Sweetheart' has been the most productive variety, keeping us well supplied from July till September with its deliciously flavoured medium sized melons. More recently we have tried to master the art of growing 'Oranje Ananas', a luxury melon (Fig. 4). It is much slower than 'Sweetheart' but, given a reasonable summer, August and September are the time for a feast. As with tomatoes I have got the best results when the plants have been fed on a high potash fertilizer.

Our cucumber needs are easily supplied by two plants; here again the results have been better when we have grown them on a mound of

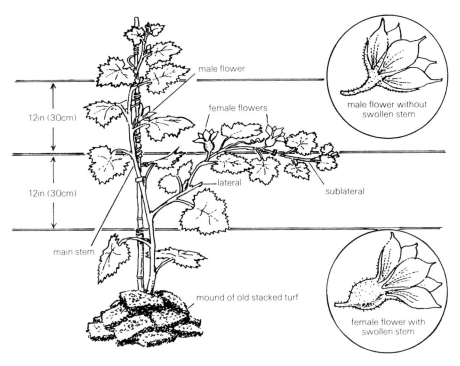

male flower

female flowers

male flower without swollen stem

12in (30cm)

lateral

sublateral

12in (30cm)

main stem

mound of old stacked turf

female flower with swollen stem

Fig. 4   Melon 'Oranje Ananas'.
I train the stem vertically and stop the leader at about 6 ft (1.8 m) to induce the production of laterals which are tied horizontally to the wires. I then pinch back each lateral at three leaves to encourage the growth of sublaterals which bear the male and female flowers. Ideally each cordon should bear six fruits and it is essential for even development that there are enough female flowers open simultaneously to obtain a set of six good fruits.

old turf. There was a time when cucumbers produced on the main stem were always bitter but since growing 'Virgo' and 'Renova' we know that it is no longer true. They are both all female flower varieties so the twice daily task of removing the male flowers is no longer necessary. Ideally cucumbers should be grown on their own but we have had to compromise by finding a shady corner for ours in with the grape vine and it has worked.

Taking delivery of a greenhouse brings with it the chance to do some gardening every day of the year. We make full use of ours and have great fun even in the dark days of winter.

THREE

Vegetables

In my opinion a well cared for and properly planned vegetable garden can not only be rewarding but extremely attractive. For instance, a row of runner beans in full flower is often just as colourful in July as some ornamental plants at that time, especially if the variety is 'Scarlet Emperor' or 'Achievement'.

For me vegetable growing has always been a challenge. First, I enjoy the cultivations involved, whereas some (and I feel sorry for them) regard the winter digging involved and the subsequent breaking up of the soil as work. If you are a real gardener it is nothing of the sort, just an enjoyable, health-giving exercise out in the fresh air. Secondly, by growing your own vegetables they come to the table fresh, full of vitamins and with no loss of the health factors *en route*. In addition and very important we select each and every vegetable variety for its edible qualities with the emphasis every time on flavour. Unlike most commercial vegetable growers we do not have to be concerned with the risk of damage in transit, shelf life or eye appeal at the point of sale. Incidentally so many of the best flavoured varieties are bad travellers and poor keepers.

Apart from all the health benefits, growing your own vegetables can be a profitable way of spending your leisure time, in fact it is impossible if your choice of varieties is right, to cost home grown vegetables as you cannot find comparable quality in the ordinary commercial market, so the results of your labour are without price, that is if you appreciate flavour in all your vegetable dishes.

The old fashioned idea of relegating a vegetable growing area to an out of sight spot, often in the shade of trees, is all wrong. If possible a full sun position is best; excessive shade results in plants being weak with elongated growth and subsequent poor cropping results. Ideally the growing area should be related in some way to the size of the family and the demands from the kitchen. In times past when families of five were about the average a 300 sq yd (250 sq m) plot was a popular size. Now, with gardens and families much smaller, plus more knowledgeable use of fertilizers etc., a much smaller plot can satisfy the vegetable needs of an average modern-day family. For three years I cultivated a mini-plot 20 × 10 ft (6 × 3 m) a mere 200 sq ft (18 sq m) of land. The first year's cropping results did surprise me as not only did this small plot almost supply our total fresh vegetable needs but when costed at local vegetable prices it returned a profit of over £50.00. To me this seemed a possible flash in the pan but by working the plot for three whole seasons on a three year crop rotation plan, it continued to live up to its first year's achievements.

Weed control

I have never been put off by the condition of a potential site, even horrible strong growing perennial weeds such as nettles, thistles, docks, couch grass, etc. with their massive underground roots do not deter me. I have learned from experience gained in taming several wilderness areas that land dug before Christmas with all its weed rubbish, roots, in fact the lot, tucked in without a trace of them showing, is the first step towards weed control and fertility. There was a time when I went to a lot of trouble picking out and burning all or nearly all the perennial weed roots but it mattered little how well the job was done, some always survived to be dealt with in the spring. No perennial weeds now survive my first season's treatment, however tough they are at the beginning; denied the opportunity to make above-ground growth, the roots soon die of sheer exhaustion. To make a good job of it I am out at least once a week during the growing season in the early spring with a Dutch hoe to catch the weed seedlings in the white thread stage.

Once we start the routine it is easy and effective, then in subsequent seasons weed control is limited to eliminating (again with a Wolf draw hoe or a Dutch hoe) the annual weeds before they seed. Having started at Clack's Farm with a load of weeds, in a wilderness no one else 27 years ago had the courage to buy, may I suggest that either a good, well-balanced spade, a Dutch hoe or a Wolf three-pronged cultivator could be one of the best presents to encourage a relative or friend to tackle their weedy vegetable plot.

Why winter digging before Christmas? Done then there is plenty of time for the frosts, snow, rains and winds to act as nature's soil conditioners. By doing the job at the right time even a heavy clay soil responds to the cultivator followed by the rake, it all goes to making the preparation of successful seed-beds and planting areas easy. (Figure 5 gives a good idea of the area involved in cultivating our fruit and vegetable garden.) Leave the digging until Easter and the turned up clay soon dries out to brick-like lumps and, worse still, after a winter of inactivity the fair weather gardener will probably fall a victim to back ache – please do not blame the gardening if this happens to you.

Starting with virgin soil would mean that for vegetable growing the fertility level should be satisfactory, those grass and weed roots will provide the fibre to keep the soil open and allow some air to gain entry. As time goes by the plant residues will break down to supply valuable plant nutrients, this means that in the first year you may not need to add anything except some garden lime for the brassicas if the soil proves to be acid. First years' results have often been described as beginner's luck, but there is no need to worry about the future if you start by obeying nature's rules.

Composting

In the wild, nature returns its foliage, dead birds and animals to the soil; nothing is wasted, consequently the soil fertility level remains almost static. By continually growing and harvesting vegetables we take away potential fertility products, so it is up to us to make good these losses otherwise cropping results will progressively deteriorate. This we do by composting vegetable waste, lawn mowings, leaves, etc. avoiding the temptation to include animal food left overs, which invariably attract rats and other vermin. In common with many gardeners we are unable to obtain farmyard manure, consequently we have to rely on our composting efforts.

By incorporating well-rotted compost during the winter digging season we have been able to raise the level of fertility and remove fears about such problems as potato eelworm. Work that we did some years ago at the Lenton Research Station clearly showed that by providing natural food (compost or farmyard manure) for the predacious fungi in the soil, they quickly increase and become active, trapping and living on any potato eelworms within reach. So on all counts compost making is good gardening; only woody materials from a garden should be committed to the bonfire and of course suspect, diseased vegetation.

Fertilizers

Whilst it is possible to grow vegetables without fertilizer applications, crop yields are considerably increased by their use. We prefer to use fertilizers based on organic ingredients, so I use PBI Back to Nature fertilizer, or fish, blood and bone. All so called balanced fertilizers supply three essential plant foods; nitrogen which is the stimulator for

Fig. 5 Plan of vegetable/fruit garden 1982, which also includes some ornamental plants.
The six vegetable plots at the top of the garden were all used in variety trials in 1982.
G.H.1 – G.H.6: greenhouses. Sizes: GH1 – GH4: 10 × 20 ft (3 × 6 m); GH5: 12 × 8 ft (3.6 × 2.4 m); GH6: 6 × 8 ft (1.8 × 2.4 m).

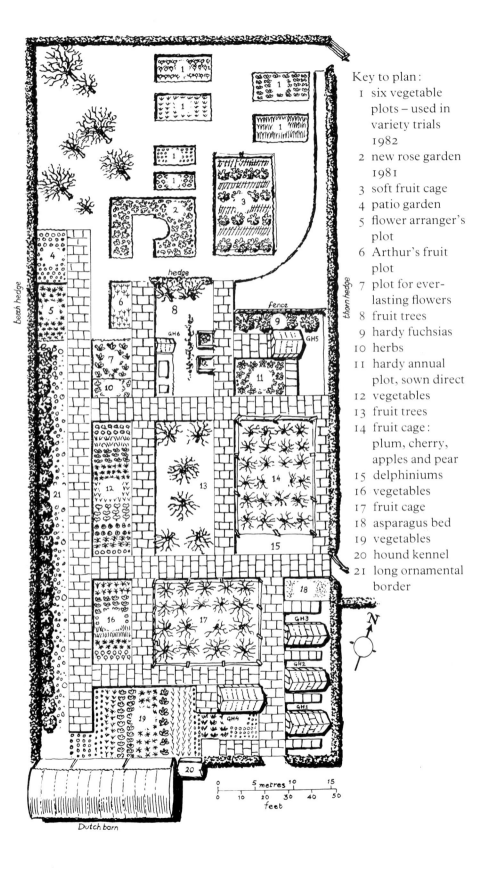

Key to plan:

1 six vegetable
  plots – used in
  variety trials
  1982
2 new rose garden
  1981
3 soft fruit cage
4 patio garden
5 flower arranger's
  plot
6 Arthur's fruit
  plot
7 plot for ever-
  lasting flowers
8 fruit trees
9 hardy fuchsias
10 herbs
11 hardy annual
  plot, sown direct
12 vegetables
13 fruit trees
14 fruit cage:
  plum, cherry,
  apples and pear
15 delphiniums
16 vegetables
17 fruit cage
18 asparagus bed
19 vegetables
20 hound kennel
21 long ornamental
  border

beech hedge

thorn hedge

hedge

fence

Dutch barn

N

0   5 metres 10   15
0 10 20 30 40 50
       feet

growth and the production of good leaf colour, phosphates which are necessary for root and seed production, and potash so necessary for plant health, good flavour and sweetness in quality varieties. However, no amount of feeding will induce flavour in a variety that has not got it naturally, the flavour factor must be there at the start.

In addition to these three major elements, some calcium in the soil is needed otherwise crops are unable to benefit to the full from any type of fertilizer treatment. However, garden lime needs to be used with discretion as excess calcium can result in iron, manganese or boron deficiencies. These and other trace elements are usually present in sufficient quantities in most garden soils, therefore the deficiencies usually occur when their uptake is interfered with by other elements, natural or unnatural. We never apply garden lime directly on to the compost or farmyard manure at the time of its incorporation into the soil; to do so would release and lose the valuable nitrogen content.

Another 'don't': never apply lime on ground scheduled for potatoes as it can cause or increase common scab on the tubers. No matter how small or large your vegetable garden, do as we do – plan it so that no crop except runner-beans is grown on the same ground more than once

FIRST YEAR	SECOND YEAR	THIRD YEAR	FOURTH YEAR
Runner beans	Runner beans	Runner beans	Runner beans
Root crops: Carrots Onions Parsnips Potatoes	*Brassicas:* Brussels sprouts Cauliflower Cabbage etc.	French beans Broad beans Peas etc.	*Root crops:* Carrots Onions Parsnips Potatoes
Brassicas: Brussels sprouts Cauliflower Cabbage etc.	French beans Broad beans Peas etc.	*Root crops:* Carrots Onions Parsnips Potatoes	*Brassicas:* Brussels sprouts Cauliflower Cabbage etc.
French beans Broad beans Peas etc.	*Root crops:* Carrots Onions Parsnips Potatoes	*Brassicas:* Brussels sprouts Cauliflower Cabbage etc.	French beans Broad beans Peas etc.

Fig. 6 My crop rotation plan for vegetables.
Note that, with the exception of the runner beans, all crops are rotated every year. Major pest and disease problems ensue if crops are not rotated.

in three years. Failure to operate a three year crop rotation (Fig. 6) sooner or later results in major pest and disease problems. It is not difficult to divide the major crops into three groups; brassicas (the cabbage family), legumes (peas and beans) and root crops which of course include potatoes. This does not mean a restriction on intercropping with quick maturing salad crops such as lettuce and radishes. Our exception to this three year rotation rule are runner beans; we site them at the north end of the plot where the shadows from their height do not create a problem.

Seed-bed preparation for any crop is easy when the soil has been winter dug and weathered, that is if you, as you should, have the patience to wait until it has dried out. Here at Clack's Farm it is usually mid-March before we can go safely on the soil. It is always fatal to trample on wet cold soil; it is a certain recipe for destroying the soil structure, which makes good gardening so difficult.

Another mistake to avoid is re-digging the ground in the spring, not only is it unnecessary but it undoes all the good achieved by weathering during the winter. My maxim is dig before Christmas and follow up with surface cultivations in early spring, that's the way to master even the most difficult soils.

Seed-bed preparation

Good results in vegetable growing begin with the preparation of the seed-bed. I start with a Wolf three-pronged cultivator to break up the overwintered clods, after that the soil dries out more quickly. A day or two later comes the next stage, further action with the cultivator and then it is up to the rake (Fig. 7) but so much depends upon the weather and the condition of the soil; sometimes it is a job spread over several days. I am never satisfied until the top tilth is fine and fairly dry; it must not stick to the tools or my boots. One of the most common mistakes is to start sowing too early, in this district the soil is seldom warm enough for good germination until the middle of March and for carrots and French beans a month later. Too-deep drilling accounts for so many complaints about poor germination. For small seeds such as onions and carrots extra care is needed, I scratch out a very shallow drill with the corner of an upturned rake, no deeper than $\frac{1}{2}$ in (1.3 cm), then when the job is finished the seed is only covered by no more than $\frac{1}{2}$ in (1.3 cm) of fine soil. I find that the little extra care pays off; I am after complete rows of seedlings without them being too close together. Overcrowding results in the individual plants struggling to survive, so sowing the seed thinly in the drill is the answer. I believe in straight rows, crooked ones make inter-row cultivations difficult so I

Fig. 7 Final preparation of the seed bed for sowing out of doors.
(*a*) Having broken down the over-wintered soil with a three-pronged cultivator, I rake the bed level, avoiding treading on the soil being prepared. (*b*) The soil is firmed by treading. (*c*) The soil is raked once more to produce a fine tilth.

always use a garden line for crops such as beetroot, carrots, onions, etc., a foot (30 cm) between each row is adequate so a 12 in (30 cm) garden rake is handy for the measuring job.

Tools

A word about tools; I am very particular about mine. For me a spade must be balanced, have a wooden shaft, have a thin sharp blade and on no account be heavy. For the last reason I have never got on well with any of the stainless steel versions. The extra weight plus a thicker blade makes more demands on the man-power. Even now with my favourite spade I have no difficulty in putting in a full day's winter digging, a wipe with a paraffin rag as it gets dusk ensures that it is bright and smiling the next morning. The same goes for my fork which is less used. Both spade and fork must be forged steel; pressed steel ones may be cheaper but I would not recommend them.

As regards the garden rake and Dutch hoe the same principles apply, for really making cultivation work easy and effective a Wolf three-pronged cultivator is a treasure. Without Wolf tools with their pull instead of push movement our 2½ acre (1 hectare) garden would have beaten Riet and I long before now. The right tools (Fig. 8) for each job make all the difference, for instance for careful weeding between rows of seedlings I use a swan necked onion hoe.

Success with vegetables

As this is not an ordinary gardening text book it is my intention to put on paper just how as a result of long experience and years of research we grow our vegetables successfully and why the end products are acclaimed to be so good.

Peas

Nothing would induce us to sow the round seeded varieties of garden peas. They certainly can be sown in the autumn or early in the season when the soil is too wet and cold for wrinkle-seeded varieties but when presented at the table they lack flavour and sweetness. Why? Because they are full of starch with very little sugar. However, we have early, quality peas by sowing 'Little Marvel' in the second half of February, all you need is a cold greenhouse, a few small pots and some seed

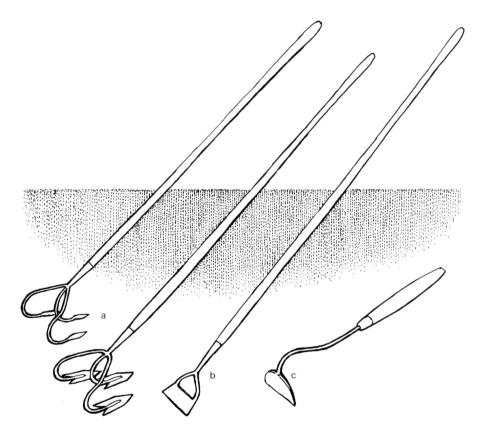

Fig. 8 Four of my most useful (post-digging) cultivation tools.
(*a*) Two types of Wolf three-pronged cultivator (*b*) Spear & Jackson Dutch hoe.
(*c*) Short handled, swan-neck onion hoe.

compost. With two seeds to a pot we are able to plant out a row of plants late March or early April, then by covering the row with cloches we bring the picking time forward by at least two weeks. Knowing that peas need a little lime I always go along the open drill with a few handfuls before planting or sowing; peas like most legumes are self sufficient as regards nitrogen, small nitrifying nodules on the roots manufacture it, so in addition to the garden lime, our peas only get a little superphosphate of lime, which can be applied at the same time as the garden lime.

Our next crop of peas comes from a row sown at the same time as when we are planting out the indoor grown plants; again I use 'Little Marvel'. Instead of making an ordinary drill I make one the width of a spade and space out the seed in rows of three. Although we have three cats, we still need to put a mouse trap under a box (Fig. 9) with a way in for the vermin, otherwise we finish up with more blanks than plants in the rows. 'Little Marvel' does not need sticks as it only reaches a height of 18 in (45 cm); it is a super cropper and any surplus to our immediate needs goes into the freezer whilst still young and tender. To follow 'Little Marvel' we sow 'Early Onward' and 'Onward', both good flavoured main crop varieties but for a September feast of garden peas we are back again to 'Little Marvel' which can be sown as late as the second half of June. All these mid-season and late peas are liable to have pea-moth maggots in the pods unless the open flowers are

Sowing garden peas. (a) In a drill the width of a spade 2 in (5 cm) deep. Each seed in the three rows is carefully spaced for economy of seed and uniform cropping. (b) The final operation — levelling the soil with a rake to ensure even germination.

a

b

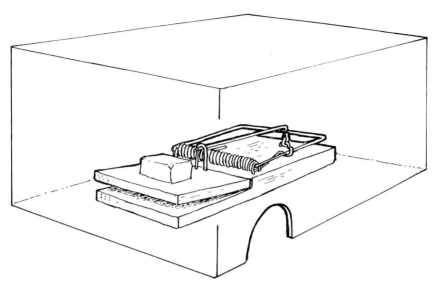

Fig. 9 The covered mouse trap. My way of ensuring that mice, indeed, are the animals which trigger the trap, and not inquisitive cats or birds.

sprayed with Derris; in addition September is mildew time so we spray with Boots systemic fungicide in August to prevent it. Until you have grown your own you just don't know how good and different garden peas can be, especially if the variety is 'Little Marvel'.

Runner beans
Runner beans are undoubtedly the most popular garden grown vegetable, no other crop can equal it for productivity in a limited space; all they need is sunshine and to have the ground well prepared. During the winter I lavish a lot of attention on the preparation of the runner-bean trench, opened up to a depth of at least a spade, I just put in a goodly amount of well-rotted compost and this I cover with a little soil to prevent it drying out. Then comes the treatment of the soil on both sides of the trench, one side gets basic slag, a slow acting phosphatic fertilizer plus trace elements, the other side receives a dressing of garden lime. If you are unable to get basic slag in your district super-phosphate of lime is a good alternative. That done the trench remains open until late March or early April; in between times nature contributes by improving the soil.

After the trench is filled in, the soil has time to settle down before planting or sowing time. As we cannot wait for the runner-bean season

a

I try to get them as early as possible, in mid-April I sow some of the seed singly in $3\frac{1}{2}$ in (9 cm) pots, little or no heat being required for germination. I use a cold greenhouse bench but a cold frame would also be right, then whilst there is still a risk of frost in mid-May I plant out, one plant to each cane but just in case the frost is too harsh for the young plants I pop a seed or two in the soil on the other side of each cane, so if the worst happens we have not lost any real time. Until recently we used the traditional system of either upright canes or bean poles in a straight row, now we have switched over to wigwams each made with four strong 8 ft (2.4 m) canes spaced about a yard (0.9 m) apart and firmly tied at the top. Cropping is even better; the beans that hang down inside under the shade of the foliage are superb, the cooler micro-climate inside the wigwam must suit them.

Generally speaking our beans are not short of moisture, the compost takes care of that, flower drop is seldom a problem but should it happen we would quickly water the row with lime water (a handful of garden lime to 2 gallons (9 litres) of water). Within three days the lime makes the phosphates in the soil available, flowers no longer drop and the beans set freely, a simple remedy which works so well that some regard it as a miracle. To ensure continuous cropping we pick regularly, if beans are allowed to get old, flower production soon comes to a halt. Our interest in runner beans is for the table rather than the show bench, so length etc. is not that important; what we want is flavour

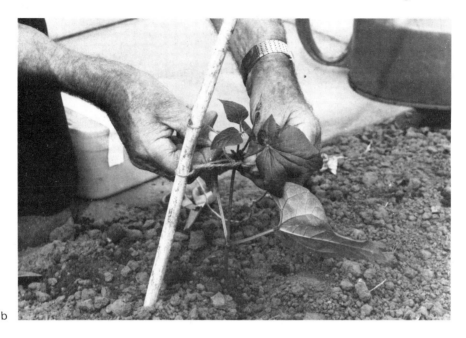

b

Planting out runner bean plants, raised in the greenhouse, in third week in May.
(**a**) Making the planting hole next to an 8 ft (2.4 m) cane. Note that the four canes
are used wigwam fashion for maximum rigidity. (**b**) The essential tie to the canes to
prevent wind damage to the tender greenhouse-produced foliage. (**c**) The author's
'belt and braces' approach; just in case of a late frost, a single seed is popped in on
the opposite side of each cane.

c

plus tenderness and 'Scarlet Emperor' our favourite has both those qualities. 'Streamline' is another good variety very similar to 'Scarlet Emperor'; 'Achievement' and 'Enorma' are long podded with quite good table qualities but for masses of shorter beans, which set freely try 'Kelvedon Marvel'.

Climbing Dutch beans and dwarf French beans

Next on my list of favourite vegetable dishes are climbing Dutch beans and it has to be the flat-podded variety 'Romore'. We grow it up cane wigwams in exactly the way we grow our runner beans and that includes the soil preparation. Whilst 'Scarlet Emperor' is still my No. 1 runner bean on account of its cropping ability, tender flesh and flavour, when sampled on the table 'Romore' is always acclaimed to be more tender and to have better flavour. No wonder it is so popular in Holland. In recent years so much emphasis has been placed on the length of the runner beans and their straightness that tenderness and flavour have almost been forgotten. However, the best of the long ones are 'Achievement', 'Enorma' and 'Streamline'. Some of the newer dwarf French beans have excellent table qualities. Here my favourites are 'Kinghorn Wax' (no good for freezing) and 'Sprite' (suitable for the freezer); both are round and stringless.

Potatoes

Having been brought up in the Fens where King Edward potatoes reigned supreme and were renowned for their quality I have always been critical about quality in potatoes. I must start with clean seed, certified by the Ministry of Agriculture, otherwise virus diseases can on occasion be so serious that the crop is hardly worth growing. I have often used potatoes as a cleaning crop on new land, there is nothing better for that job than the cultivations necessary for growing potatoes; they certainly get rid of the perennial weeds. On regularly cropped ground I have never planted potatoes more frequently than once in three years and I always put plenty of well-rotted compost in the planting trench, this is the way to prevent potato eelworm becoming a problem. To get the most out of the crop I scatter some PBI Back-to-Nature fertilizer in the open trench. I endeavour to get delivery of my seed potatoes in February, then there is plenty of time to set them up in trays to sprout, which accelerates the rate of growth after planting and increases the yield.

Maybe I am liberal with the row spacings, 2 ft 3 in (70 cm) for first earlies and 2 ft 9 in (85 cm) for main crop varieties; closer planting only reduces the yield and the number of large potatoes per root. Planting

a

Planting potatoes.
(**a**) With line and spade the trench is opened up for a row of first early 'Duke of York' potatoes. (**b**) Applying PBI Back to Nature fertilizer along the line of a trench to help ensure a good quality crop. (**c**) Spacing the tubers with the sprouts pointing upwards, along the trench. On each potato the number of sprouts has been reduced to three.

b

c

time with us starts when the soil is ready; in some seasons it may be as late as mid-March or even later. It would always be a mistake to start planting whilst the ground was still wet and cold. The wider spacing makes earthing up easier with less disturbance of the feeding roots; without earthing up some of the potatoes would be pushed out into the daylight, become green and virtually useless. By the way I never like to earth up potatoes with dry soil, once earthed up it takes an enormous amount of rain before any of it reaches the roots.

Potatoes are frost sensitive so in May when the nights can be cold and frosty I often find it wise to draw some soil up and cover the rapidly growing tops, when they are too tall for this I use several layers of newspaper weighted down with a stone or two, uncovering them each morning. Large glass-covered cloches are a great help provided the foliage does not touch the glass; on occasion when I have used plastic-covered cloches, the damage underneath them has been greater than on the potatoes with no protection at all.

Ideas about potatoes vary considerably. At Clack's Farm 'Duke of York' is our favourite first early, it is an old re-invigorated variety with a flavour that is for most people unfortunately only a memory. For those who like a slightly more moist flesh potato 'Manna', a newcomer to the market, is excellent and it bulks somewhat quicker than 'Duke of York'. The U.K. insistence on white-fleshed potatoes is now fading, simply because the continental varieties with creamy or yellow flesh have more flavour. 'Desiree' a red-skinned potato with creamy flesh seems to have broken down much of the resistance, consequently the even better flavoured 'Diana', 'Altena' and 'Fanfare' should not be delayed too long before gaining popularity. The more potato trials I carry out the more convinced I am that good flavour is synonymous with creamy or yellow fleshed varieties.

I cannot understand why gardeners bother to grow 'Arran Pilot', 'Majestic' and some of the other white-fleshed varieties; maybe they are still good enough for chips but such a lot has happened in the plant breeding world since they were introduced.

For three years running we have enjoyed new, easy to scrape potatoes for Christmas Day lunch; to achieve this we hold back a few sprouted seed, keeping them in good light under a greenhouse bench until early July. In 1981 we planted Fanfare on the 2nd of July; they were up in a week, earthed up a fortnight later and when we lifted the first root on November 8th we were more than surprised by the weight – it was slightly over $6\frac{1}{2}$ lb (3 kg). Incidentally that was the severe winter of 1981/1982; we were not able to dig on Christmas Day that year but by early February, after days at $-24°C$, we were once again

The busy season, early April, in the 20 × 10 ft (6 × 3 m) Alton cedarwood greenhouse. The benches are packed with half hardy seedlings. Note the Humex electric fan heater on the shelf, which comes into action if the temperature falls below 50°F. An economic Heatmor 10 ft (3 m) paraffin water heater supplies the basic heating.

Glorious colour in July. Our Robinson aluminium 20 × 10 ft (6 × 3 m) greenhouse filled with streptocarpus, begonias and geraniums, all raised at Clack's Farm.

Above: The vegetable plot in August. The author with a trug basket full of fresh, full flavoured produce for the kitchen.

Left: Morello cherries at the brilliant red fruit stage, before turning black and becoming fully ripe. They are trained on a fence, and within a fruit cage to defeat the birds.

digging and enjoying new potatoes, thanks to the 10 in (25 cm) of snow only the odd potato was frozen. Whilst 'Fanfare' gave us this record crop I have in previous seasons been well satisfied with a number of other varieties especially 'Desiree' which seems to be well suited for the job. We always have some late potatoes to store and I still prefer to put them in an old fashioned clamp (Fig. 10), covered with straw and soil they keep stored so much better this way than in a sack or box, not surprising as a clamp is much closer to nature's own method.

Carrots
Whilst carrots always do best on light to medium types of soil, thorough winter digging can produce good results on some of the heavier soils. I avoid sowing carrots on ground recently treated with compost or manure, too rich a soil results in a lot of forked roots. Neither do I sow carrots before April, by then the soil is beginning to warm up. A very shallow drill and a steady hand is needed otherwise too much seed is sown, which means thinning and a greater risk of carrot fly damage. We are in a carrot fly area but Bromophos granules in the open seed drill and Fisons Combat sprayed on to the seedlings at the first true leaf stage keep ours clean. One other golden rule, do not start sowing until you have prepared a really good seed-bed.

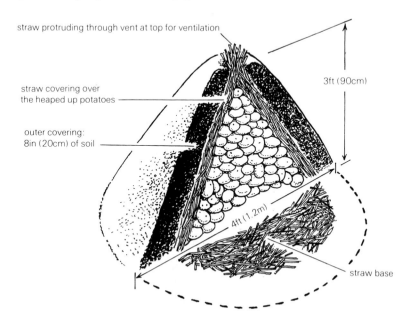

straw protruding through vent at top for ventilation

3ft (90cm)

straw covering over
the heaped up potatoes

outer covering:
8in (20cm) of soil

4ft (1.2m)

straw base

Fig. 10   Construction of a potato clamp, still, in my view, the best way to store potatoes. Note that ventilation is provided by the straw vent at the top of the clamp.

During the season I make several successional sowings so we have young carrots throughout the season. In June I sow my maincrop for use during the winter. Carrots from this latter sowing are less subject to splitting which can be a problem once the autumn rains begin. On heavy clay soils carrots must be lifted for storing but like potatoes they do keep best in a clamp covered with straw and soil. Other methods are recommended but more often than not the carrots either dry out or go rotten. In our medium type soil I let them stay put in the row where they keep in perfect condition until April, after that regrowth starts.

As the result of some very successful plant breeding hard yellow cores in carrots have disappeared, instead some newer varieties have practically no core, and super flavoured, red and tender flesh. For our first sowing it is 'Amsterdam Forcing'; it is usually ready for pulling in 12 to 16 weeks, a great carrot when young. Then for one to follow I like 'Asmer New Model'; it is a good choice for successive sowings during the summer but for my main crop, for winter use, it's 'Chantenay Red Cored' ('Asmer Red Coat') – it can cope with heavy frosts. If I was faced with a shallow heavy soil I would grow 'Cluseed New Stump Rooted'.

Parsnips

A vegetable with no storage problems is the parsnip, in fact it always improves in flavour and tenderness after a good frost, ours stay in the ground until wanted but I sometimes lift a few roots on the top just in case of a frost severe enough to freeze the ground solid. According to many books, February is parsnip-sowing time but for me it is March; parsnip seed is slow to germinate and can rot easily if the soil is cold and damp. To get over this delay I chit the seed first by putting it between a couple of layers of damp cloth or blotting paper, keeping it damp all the time at room temperature. After about ten days the seed has swollen with the first signs of germination appearing, this is the time I trust the seed to the soil, three seeds to each position in the row 9 in (23 cm) apart, again only covering them with $\frac{1}{2}$ in ($1\frac{1}{4}$ cm) of fine soil. When the seedlings are well established with signs of the first true leaves, I thin out leaving the strongest looking one in each position. A well prepared deep soil is best without any recent compost treatment, if during the growing season the plants seem to need an encouraging feed I give ours a foliar feed. On some soils parsnip canker can be a problem and the roots start to rot at the shoulder; there is no known cure, a slight injury when hoeing can start it. If canker is your problem try sowing later with either the short rooted variety 'Avonresistor' or 'Asmer Improved Marrow', which has longer roots.

Onions

For me growing onions always has been and still is a challenge. Success with the crop is not gained easily, maybe that is why the large show onions always attract so much attention; it certainly requires expertise and experience to produce those 5–6 lb (2.3–2.7 kg) onions. However, I have never wished to exhibit on the show bench but I must say that a recent crop of Robinson's 'Improved Mammoth' with some turning the scale at 5 lb 6 oz (2.4 kg) did a lot to boost my ego, I am now trying to do even better with 'Lancastrian'. No outdoor vegetable crop is more responsive to good treatment than onions, so much depends on the preparation of the ground before sowing or planting. Some devotees use the same spot for their onion bed each season, building up the fertility by piling in masses of compost or well rotted manure each winter. However, sooner or later white rot, a fungus disease, creeps in and the site has to be changed.

I prefer to stick to a crop rotation plan with onions following peas and beans, then during the winter the best compost I can find goes in, the digging being done with a full sized spade, not one of my well worn shorties. During the winter the soil settles down, well weathered by frost, winter rains and winds. In the New Year as soon as it is dry enough I start the clod breakdown process with my favourite three pronged cultivator; I like a firm onion bed with a friable soil on top, this takes time to achieve, more action with the cultivator and finally with the rake. During these operations I apply PBI Back-to-Nature fertilizer which onions seem to like. By late March or early April I am usually satisfied that all is ready.

For the larger onions which I really grow for fun, I sow the seed in the greenhouse on Christmas Day, and for them I start up a small Ward electric propagator which is automatically controlled at 62°F (17°C), I prick out the seedlings at the loop stage into $3\frac{1}{2}$ in (8 cm) pots, using Levington potting compost, then round about the second week in April I plant them out 10 in (25 cm) apart. They seem to stand still for a while but during that time the roots are going down deeply into the compost-enriched soil. Once above-ground growth starts it is action every week with the fertilizer bag, little and often is the rule, until August ripening off time. The larger the onions the more important it is to make sure that they are really ripe and thoroughly dried before storing in a dry and airy place.

Apart from the onions grown for fun, which do not keep too well, I grow onions for the kitchen and these need to be so good that they can be kept till the next harvest comes again. The choice is wide but growing from sets is the most popular method. I grow two varieties

Planting onion sets ('Sturon') with a trowel. After firming with the fingers, only the tip of the onion sets show above ground.

'Stuttgarter Giant' and 'Sturon'; planting time for me is April since if it is done any earlier they tend to bolt to seed. After removing any excess dead top on the set I plant with a trowel and I plant so that only the very tip of the set can be seen. If you press the sets into the soil the roots push them up and out and if you leave the dead tops on the birds pull them out. For onion sets a fertilizer feed once a month is sufficient. As with all onions I keep the bed weed free; no onions do well with weeds competing for food, water and light.

The traditional method of sowing onion seed direct involves the risk of onion fly – here again I use Bromophos in the open drill and Fisons Combat two or three weeks after germination. Onion seed is expensive so I am naturally careful to sow thinly but apart from this I never like to thin out or pull spring onions from an ordinary onion bed as the smell of bruised onions attracts the fly. We find that direct sown onions are the best keepers, especially if we sow varieties such as 'Rijnsburger' or 'Asmer Lancastrian', which are far superior to some of the older varieties such as 'Bedfordshire Champion' for instance. If the weather and soil conditions are right I get on with the sowing in late March but I am always prepared to wait a week or two for really good seed-bed conditions. Not wishing to get very big onions I limit the fertilizer applications to once a month, with a complete ban on feeding from the beginning of August.

Ripening onions for storing in a good season with dry soil conditions and sunshine is relatively easy; in a cold and wet season it can be

Using the onion hoe with great care between transplanted 'Lancastrian' onions in May, one month after they were planted out in April, 10 in (25 cm) apart.

difficult. The secret is the timing to lift – no need to bend the tops over they will go over naturally when ready – the onion must be mature and beginning to ripen naturally, and the first sign of this process is drying off. I lift ours on to the concrete slab path; they stand there for a few days before going either into the scullery where the central heating boiler maintains a dry atmosphere or on to the greenhouse bench (p. 40); it is this quick drying off that does the trick. After that we string them up in ropes and store them in an airy, frost-free lean-to building. A dusting with flowers of sulphur or green sulphur does help to prevent storage rots but the real secret is to keep the onions dry.

For salad onions we sow at the same time 'White Lisbon' but on account of onion fly as far away from the main crop as possible. For good keeping onions with little or no ripening problems I grow the so-called Japanese onions which, sown in August, ripen in June, a time when the days are long and the nights free from dew. With varieties such as 'Express Yellow' and 'Senshyu' we have been very successful with no over-winter plant losses. However, the sowing date is critical; here in Worcestershire sowing time is the third week in August, in more northern parts of England and in Scotland it would have to be done during the first week in August whilst in south Wales and southern England sowing can be delayed until the first week in September. Apart from a straight sulphate of ammonia feed early in the New Year to cheer them up after the winter I treat them in the same way as all other onions.

The crop of 'Lancastrian' onions drying out on the greenhouse bench (September). Average weight 3½ lb (1.58 kg). Note the fan 'heater' under bench, used to blow cold air to maintain air circulation.

Shallots

For pickling we always have plenty of suitable small onions but for really superb solid pickling onions it is difficult to beat shallots, either 'Giant Yellow' or 'Giant Red', so I still follow the old time practice of planting on the shortest day and lifting ripe on the longest day. I plant with a trowel at the very end of the vegetable plot without treading on the wet December soil; for this our concrete paths are very convenient.

Leeks

For a truly reliable winter vegetable, leeks are our sure standby, they are always there ready for the pot. It takes a long time to grow good leeks even the moderate sized ones for the kitchen. I start by sowing the seed outside in March or April, the plants are then ready for planting out in June. In common with their relatives the onions they appreciate good treatment, I start by digging out a trench the width and depth of a spade, and fork into the bottom some very good compost, this is a job I like to get done well ahead of planting time. For planting I use an old fashioned dibber, a bit like a cut down garden fork shaft with a pointed end, with it I make holes into the bottom of the trench 4 or 5 in (10–12 cm) deep and 9 in (23 cm) apart. The planting operation is simple. I drop the plants singly into the holes, then give each one a little water which washes down some soil around the roots and that is the end of the job. As the leeks grow I draw in gradual stages the soil up around them until the trench is filled and then finally some earthing up completes the stem blanching process. Whilst this is going on over a period of weeks I work in some fertilizer, a couple of applications of PBI Back to Nature or Fisons Vegetable Fertilizer. We have no storage problem for the winter, leeks are simply left in the ground and lifted when needed in the kitchen. If the forecast is frost I sometimes lift a few and heel them in in a sheltered spot.

Brassicas

Brassicas, especially Brussels sprouts, cauliflowers and cabbages, are such useful vegetables that there will always be a temptation to devote more than a third of the plot to them. To do this would defeat any crop rotation plan and sooner or later result in dire consequences including club root. To maintain strictly a three year crop rotation means that any of the brassicas should not be grown in one position on the plot more than once in three years. All brassicas do best on land that has been dug some months previously and has had time to settle down. In other words, if possible, do not plant on recently dug ground. If you have to, trample it well before planting; all brassicas like the ground to be firm. Another point, brassicas do not appreciate very acid soil, here at Clack's Farm I always apply garden lime to the area scheduled for them. Whilst lime will not control club root it does help to prevent it. I make it a golden rule to grow all my own brassica plants from seed, when you buy or accept plants as a gift you can so easily introduce this dreaded disease, and once club root is introduced into a soil, a lifetime is not long enough to get rid of it.

Apart from spring cabbages I sow most of the other main crop brassicas towards the end of March or early April, a seed-bed with short rows provides all the plants I need. It is no wonder that the wise old gardeners considered Easter just about the right time to bring out their hand cultivators and the garden rakes, there are still no better tools for getting a good seed-bed tilth. It is often necessary here to do the job in stages, I like the wind to give some help with the final drying processes to get the tilth just right. For brassicas I make a routine practice of raking in a little garden lime whilst preparing the seed-bed; apart from anything else it certainly improves the colour of the seedlings' foliage.

Brussels sprouts. As with most people Brussels sprouts are a must and now with F_1 hybrids available the plants are more uniform and, if we choose the right varieties, the cropping can be so much better, in addition the buttons are of a more even size, easier to pick and if need be stay on the stems for a much longer period without rotting. Having tried many I have no hesitation in recommending a few including U.K. bred varieties.

For the small garden where space is at a premium 'Peer Gynt' is always a good choice; it is dwarf, consequently standing up well in exposed situations. It is ready for picking in October and November. Then for December and the traditional Christmas Day lunch we have a number of quality varieties, one being 'Perfect Line' which, although taller than 'Peer Gynt', is shorter than most mid-season varieties. 'Achilles', one of my favourites, in common with 'Aries' are real winter varieties, their uniform quality sprouts will stay put for weeks on the stems without spoiling, even in frosty weather. Personally I am not keen on cooked sprout tops but if you are then 'Ormavon' would be a good one to grow, its tops are larger than any others – they look somewhat like cabbages on top of sprout stems.

Not being plagued with club root I cannot confirm the claims that 'Leander', a mid-season variety, is somewhat resistant to the disease but for the less fortunate it might be worth trying. F_1 hybrid seed is expensive; so called three- and four-way hybrid seed is less costly to produce and in this group I have found 'Troika' well suited to our needs for cropping ability and quality of sprouts. I have given up growing open-pollinated varieties as they suffer from too much variation in type and quality.

Cabbages. When it comes to cabbages and cauliflowers it is a different story, F_1 hybrids mature within the rows on almost the same day and without cutting quickly they go to waste. This is ideal for the commercial grower; the whole crop can be harvested in one go but for the household gardener it is better to have one cabbage or cauliflower ready at a time, with the rest coming along over a period of days or even weeks. This is why I prefer to start the season with a sowing of 'Greyhound Cabbage' rather than the F_1 'Hispi'. I admit that 'Hispi' is a fast growing, excellent pointed cabbage but the moment it is ready it cracks and that is the end. However, if I sow 'Greyhound' in February in the greenhouse and plant it out in April, it may come a week later but the cutting of sound cabbages goes on and keeps the kitchen supplied for several weeks.

I still grow that classic summer cabbage 'Winningstadt', if well grown every one becomes capable of winning a prize, and its solid, well-blanched hearts never fail to please a good cook. I sow the seed in March or early April for it to be ready for cutting in August/September. Whereas 'Winningstadt' makes a large pointed cabbage, 'Buderich' is almost round headed and it is our October cabbage. Then for the winter we do sow F_1 hybrids as varieties of the Savoy type such as 'Celtic', which will stand for a long time without spoiling. We have also found 'Aquarius' excellent; it makes medium-sized, lightly packed heads and in common with 'January King' it is able to stand the rigours of winter.

Although I am not fond of pickles in any form I do grow just a few red cabbage. Riet's choice is 'Langendijk Red Medium', it certainly looks a good colour when shredded in vinegar. Boiled red cabbage is one of Riet's favourite dishes, which I go along with if the helping is small; it certainly is a winter vegetable with a difference and could with advantage be more popular in this country.

For spring cabbage I make a point of sowing the seed early in August, for planting out on ground cleared of potatoes. I have tried numerous varieties including 'April' which makes a very tender small cabbage, 'Offenham' is much larger and a little later. More recently I have grown a new one 'Dorado' which has an unequalled growth rate in the spring and that is the time when fresh vegetables are always in short supply.

Cauliflowers. Cauliflowers can be disappointing as a crop unless the growing snags are appreciated and avoided. On no account should cauliflowers have a growth check; if it occurs early, maturing follows with 'buttons' instead of large cauliflower curds. To prevent buttoning either sow the seed direct in the row and thin out the plants to 2 ft (60 cm) apart, or transplant from the seed-bed before a growth check occurs and keep the plants on the move by watering and feeding. In addition take positive steps to control cabbage root fly: (1) sprinkle Bromophos in the open seed drill; (2) water transplants with dilute Fisons Combat; and (3) immediately after planting put a Secto brassica collar around each single plant.

Whilst a straight nitrogen fertilizer such as sulphate of ammonia or nitrochalk is excellent for feeding most brassicas, for cauliflowers I prefer to use a balanced fertilizer such as Growmore, which gives me a whiter curd than just plain nitrogen.

The variety 'All the Year Round – Leo' is my stand by, I sow it for succession throughout the season, starting first in the greenhouse in early March in peat pots and finishing with a direct sown row in June.

For an earlier crop we have been very satisfied with 'Mechelse Cluseed Major' sown in the greenhouse in January. Grown well 'Flora Blanca' is the one to win a red card with at the local September show but it does need a little expertise on the way. For winter cauliflowers to mature in April I have stuck to 'Walcheren Winter' as in our district only the truly hardy varieties survive.

Sprouting broccoli. We grow purple sprouting broccoli although it virtually occupies the ground for 12 months; on the other hand calabrese 'Express Corona' sown in March crops in August/September and is even more delicious, but to make the most of it you must cut the centre and side shoots young and never allow any to go to seed, which they do quickly.

Celery. I am particularly fond of celery but it must be crisp and sweet, qualities not found in any of the self-blanching varieties, so I am still growing our celery in the traditional way. Planted in a trench with plenty of compost worked in the bottom and earthed up as it grows, it really does produce the long blanched sticks without that stringy fibre, the nutty flavoured celery to enjoy with a piece of cheese. For October/November 'Solid White' is the variety of my choice, with a row of 'Giant Red' a more hardy variety to carry us on into the New Year. For soups and stews I grow celeriac, it does not need earthing up. The variety 'Balder' has given us good, well shaped turnip-like roots with plenty of celery flavour.

It is this insistence on quality and flavour that makes every main meal at Clack's Farm a time when we say 'thank goodness we grow all our own vegetables'.

FOUR

Fruit

It is easy to lay down hard and fast rules for successful fruit growing but in small gardens it is not always possible to comply with them. However, with forethought there are few situations that cannot be somewhat improved and the risks of disappointments reduced.

For all fruits the land needs to be well drained, it would be folly to plant on a site subject either to regular flooding or waterlogging. In addition frost pockets should be avoided or if possible dealt with in such a way that the cold night air during a spring frost can flow away downhill. It is this cold air build up during a spring frost that causes blossom damage and the closer the blossom is to the ground the greater the risk.

Frost and drainage problems

When prospecting in search of land for the Thurgarton Fruit Research Unit I turned down several fields in the district simply because in no way would it be possible to solve the frost pocket problems. The offer of 'The Hollows', a smallholding with its four small fields was different, here we could deal with the cold air flow problem as the whole area was on a south-facing slope (Fig. 11). Beyond the lower boundary hedge there was a sheer drop of 10 ft (3 m) or more to the road which was also falling away quickly downhill. With the decision taken I decided to lower all the hedges to ensure an unimpeded cold air flow; the success was such that in twenty years we did not have a single spring frost disaster, which meant consistently good crops.

As the land was very heavy clay with reputation for winter flooding we undertook a pre-planting drainage scheme which involved laying down a carefully planned network of clay land tiles (drain pipes), laid in trenches on coarse washed gravel; the outflow of water went into newly cleaned-out ditches. I mention this experience as it was an opportunity for me to demonstrate that in a non-recognized fruit district, on land that the locals frowned upon for fruit growing, a site could be developed for continuously successful growing. In our case the loss of crops for any reason would have meant the loss of a whole year's research work and that would have been even more serious than a season without crops for an ordinary fruit grower.

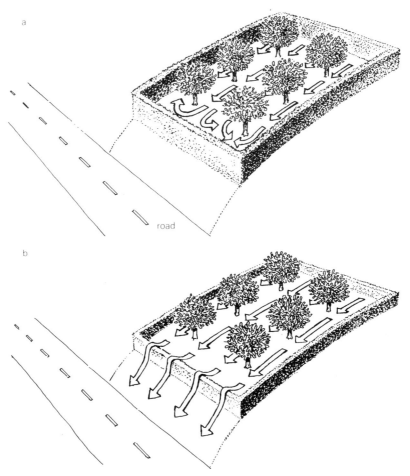

Fig. 11 Solving a frost pocket problem.
(*a*) Cold air, flowing downhill, is retained by the high 8½ ft (2.55 m) hedges, leading to frost-damaged fruit trees. (*b*) By cutting back the hedges to a 5 ft (1.5 m) height, the cold air is able to flow away downhill more freely.

Due to the much higher land to the east our fruit at Clack's Farm has always been at some risk but fortunately our adjacent fields slope gently away to the west and towards the river Severn. It is 15 years since we started fruit growing and we now have a classic example of how the planting of a beech hedge around a garden increases spring frost hazards. For purposes of television we needed a 6 ft (1.8 m) background hedge and recently we have noted an increase in spring frost blossom damage especially on strawberries, so reluctantly we have lowered the hedge to about 4 ft (1.2 m). It is this type of approach that can help to ease frost problems in small gardens. I have known cases where garden gates left open at night have done the trick, all we have to appreciate is that cold air flows downhill like water and that if possible we must give it an opportunity to get away.

Planting

With these considerations taken into account I make sure that the ground is thoroughly dug over before planting. In the case of soft fruit I insist on the land being absolutely clean and free from perennial weed roots, even if it means a year's delay. For me fruit tree planting is a job for November and I want my young trees to be maidens (one year olds), lifted and supplied direct from the nursery with bare roots. Why maidens? Well, I find that not only do they cost less than older trees but they settle down and get away far more quickly. Why November? In November the trees are dormant and are less easily damaged. On arrival the sooner they are planted the better; however, if, for various reasons immediate planting is out of the question, I lay them in the soil with their roots well covered until it is possible to plant.

Container grown trees are usually more expensive but the convenience of being able to collect them from the garden centre and plant them at any time of the year is an obvious attraction. However there are disadvantages especially when they are planted during the growing season, a time when the ball of roots within the compost should not be disturbed. I like to plant trees with their roots spaced out, clean cut root ends just before planting (Fig. 12) ensures healthy new root growth and a subsequent root lay-out as nature intended, whereas container grown trees tend to develop roots going round and round in circles without venturing far afield. Another out-of-season container planting problem is the need for frequent watering until re-establishment is complete, I have found that container compost always dries out more quickly than the soil around it.

In my experience fruit trees get off the mark more quickly when planted without rich manures or compost in the planting holes, a handful of sterilized bonemeal is my limit. The time to consider feeding is after the trees have settled down and have new roots capable of utilizing the nutrients.

Rootstocks: apples

Gone are the days when apples were generally grafted or budded on vigorous rootstocks, for me picking apples perched high up on a long ladder is out, so the type of rootstock on which a tree has been budded or grafted is all important. So much research and development has gone into the selection and knowledge of rootstock performances that

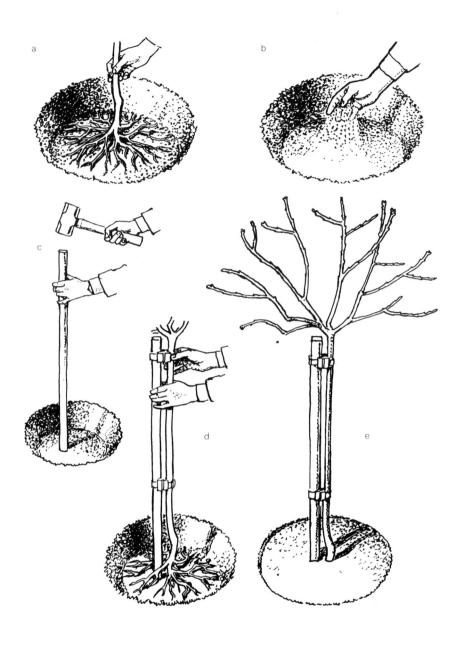

Fig. 12 Planting a young fruit tree

(a) Dig a hole sufficiently deep so that the grafting point will be well above the soil level and sufficiently wide so that the roots can be spread out. (b) Add a single handful of bone meal. (c) Set a stake in the hole before planting the tree – the stake should be on the windward side of the tree. (d) Set the tree against the stake and secure the tree to the stake by two tree ties. (e) Refill hole with soil, ensuring there are no empty air pockets left between the roots, and that the top surface is level.

for me I must know the full details. A bare statement on the label that it is on a dwarfing rootstock tells me nothing, apple rootstocks are numerous but for the gardener I would suggest the following:

> Malling 9, a truly dwarfing rootstock suitable for good soils. At Clack's Farm dwarf bush and cordons have done particularly well on it, they have cropped early some even in their first year, which is not generally recommended. One snag with this rootstock is that the roots are fibrous and brittle, so it is necessary to provide anchorage by efficient tying and staking throughout the whole life of the tree.
> Malling 26 is slightly more vigorous and could do better than Malling 9 on light poorer soils; it also needs permanent staking.
> MM 106 is a semi-dwarfing rootstock bred for its resistance to woolly aphid. On our soil it is too vigorous for either cordons or dwarf bush trees, consequently presents excessive pruning problems.

Whilst with dwarfing rootstocks it is possible to reduce planting distances it is still wise to be fairly generous: for Malling 9, I allow 13 ft (4 m), for Malling 26, 18 ft (5.4 m) and for MM 106, 20 ft (6 m); our cordons on Malling 9 are planted 3 ft (90 cm) apart in the row.

Perhaps before moving on I should mention that Malling 9 rootstock is not too popular in the garden nursery trade, simply because at the point of sale being such a small tree, it does not compare favourably with trees on the more vigorous rootstocks, but for me its cropping behaviour is far more important.

Rootstocks: pears, plums and cherries

The choice of suitable rootstocks for pears and plums is more limited. There are at least two proven rootstocks for pears:

> Quince A, this is semi-vigorous and can therefore be expected to make a sizeable tree and it should be remembered that pears do not enjoy being pruned. On this rootstock most varieties will be a few years old before cropping really begins.
> Quince C is semi-dwarfing therefore it is my choice for any garden, either for growing as cordons or dwarf bushes, although it does need permanent support.

For plums my choice is St. Julian A which is semi-dwarfing. Myrobalan is a vigorous rootstock favoured here in Worcestershire for damsons which by nature are not very vigorous.

We had high hopes for the new Colt dwarfing rootstock for cherries grown in fruit cages but on our soil it has proved more vigorous than expected, so gone are our hopes of plentiful cherry crops in years to come. Without protection we would only get those the birds left for us and even then in a few years' time it could well be a ladder-picking job.

Climate

Gardens 600 ft (180 m) or more above sea-level and those within 5 miles (8 km) of the coast are not really suitable for tree fruit growing. The amount of rainfall is important, although there are few districts in the country with an annual average below 24 in (0.4 m) which is regarded as the minimum. However, in the low-rainfall areas, artificial watering during dry periods can help to increase fruit size and crop yields. In high-rainfall districts the problems are different; many of the better dessert apples such as 'Cox's Orange Pippin' become difficult, quality certainly deteriorates and diseases like apple and pear scab become more troublesome, especially in the warmer spring and summer areas of the country.

For the best quality dessert apples, pears and plums, summer sunshine and warmth are needed. Apples are more tolerant of cold growing conditions than pears, a reason why the latter always do best in the south-eastern counties.

Apricots, peaches and nectarines all need more sunshine and warmth during the outdoor growing season than we normally get in Worcestershire, maybe in more favoured districts they are worth trying. Even so, to get worthwhile results planting in front of a south or west facing fence or wall is advisable, plus some protection against frost in late February or early March, the normal blossom time. In addition peach leaf curl is an ever recurring problem on outdoor trees.

Raspberries and most other cane fruits revel in moist growing conditions, hence the reason why some of the finest raspberries are produced in Scotland. Strawberries can be grown almost everywhere but in the wetter districts botrytis (grey mould) on the ripening berries is a problem. 'Royal Sovereign', the most susceptible variety, should certainly be avoided; fortunately there are less susceptible varieties.

Drainage

The need for good drainage has already been mentioned. Light and gravelly soils will naturally have good drainage. On medium soils overlying gravel or rock, except in low lying areas, drainage is usually satisfactory. The real drainage problems occur on heavier soils overlying clay where the water in the sub-soil is unable to get away. In addition heavy soils overlying chalk or calcareous gravel are often after a few years subject to trace element deficiencies, especially iron, which show up as chlorosis in the foliage. The ideal and easy fruit growing soil types are definitely within the medium soil ranges where the top soil is deep and the natural fertility is high, then by good management fruit growing is not likely to be difficult.

A nine-year-old James Grieve dwarf bush apple tree on Malling 9 rootstock in full bloom, spring 1982. The result in September was nearly 100 lb (45 kg) of delicious dessert apples.

Two large old 'Clapps Favourite' pear trees in full blossom provide the back cloth. In left foreground is a row of cordon apples on Malling 9 rootstock, behind which are our compost bins. In right mid-ground is a recently sown annual flower seed plot.

Above: A trial plot of 26 Lincolnshire grown daffodil varieties in its second season. In left foreground is 'Magnificence', the earliest yellow trumpet daffodil, next to them 'Ice Follies', the author's favourite.

Left: A birthday present from my daughter Margaret, presented in June 1982, ready planted with 'Blue Joy' petunias and 'Queen Sophia' marigolds.

Lighter and gravelly soils are by nature hungry as nutrients are more quickly leached away beyond the reach of the roots, consequently there is always a greater need for regular feeding plus application of organic matter such as well-rotted compost or manure to hold the nutrients at reachable depths for the roots. Trees standing in ground subject to water-logging suffer in severe cases from root die back and canker is usually a recurring problem on poorly drained land. It is pointless to lay either drainage pipes or underground rubble tracks if the water is unable to get right away from the site. Nor is there any useful purpose served by filling in planting holes with lighter soil, in fact that often increases the problem of stagnant water round the roots.

Cordons

For the garden where space is at a premium and several varieties are involved, cordons (Fig. 13) are the obvious answer especially for

Fig. 13   Fruit trees: cordon.
(*a*) A cordon apple shcwing correct planting angle. (*b*) A row of cordon apples showing the supporting framework with shoots tied to bamboo canes. Note the blossom on short spurs on the lower parts of the cordons.

apples. Planted 3 ft (0.9 m) apart, grown on single stems, sloping at an angle of 45° and supported by posts and wires, most varieties except the tip bearers such as 'Worcester Pearmain' and 'Discovery', are easy to manage providing they are on Malling 9 or Malling 26 rootstocks. The reason for planting at an angle of 45° is the need to slow down the sap flow; this results in more fruit spur production and less extensive leaf growth. For support I have used stout angle-iron stakes but 2 × 2 in (5 × 5 cm) oak ones are a good alternative provided they are treated with a horticultural wood preservative (not creosote). In either case I want them to be 18 in (45 cm) in the ground and 5 ft (1.5 m) above to carry three strands of wire equally spaced.

When planting I first tie in a sloping 6 ft (1.8 m) cane at each position and after planting tie the tree stem fairly loosely to the canes using soft fillis string, too tight tying or the use of hard nylon string would soon lead to the string cutting into the swelling stem with dire consequences. If at all possible I like the cordons to slope away from the sun so that when in fruit it all gets the maximum amount of sunshine. In the case of double rows a 6 ft (1.8 m) space between would be my recommendation. Pruning cordon apples is done twice a year, once in late July or early August and again in November or before the end of February. Too early summer pruning must be avoided otherwise buds intended for fruiting the following season will break into immediate growth, this results in little or no crop the following year.

Pears can be grown as cordons but are somewhat less amenable to the hard pruning cordon growing demands, the only rootstock suitable in my opinion is Quince C. However, at Clack's Farm 'Williams Bon Chrétien', 'Conference', 'Onward', 'Louise Bonne de Jersey' and 'Doyenné du Comice' have cropped fairly consistently, planted together they take care of each others' pollination problems. The secret with both apples and pears is to plant varieties that blossom at the same time. Incidentally we used to regard 'James Grieve' as the best pollinator for 'Cox's Orange Pippin' but now our choice is 'Discovery', that wonderful coloured late August apple.

Red or white currants and gooseberries are ideal subjects for growing as cordons, not only do they crop quality fruit every year but grown in single closely pruned rows the netting against birds is so much easier. The method of planting is the same as for cordon trees but the distance between each single stem can be 18 in (45 cm)

Espaliers and fan trained trees
Both systems (Fig. 14) are suitable for a garden with a wall or fence facing either south or west and in common with cordons take up little

space for growing top quality fruit. An espalier is trained so that the well-spaced branches grow out from the main stem at right angles whereas, as the name implies, a fan trained tree is virtually a living fan with its branches radiating from the base. In both cases the pruning is carried out twice a year as suggested for cordons.

Family trees

These are available as bush trees on 2–3 ft (0.6–0.9 m) stems with three varieties grafted on to a single tree. The pollination problem is then solved, particularly if you have only space for one tree. There are five different combinations of apple varieties to choose from but only one selection of pear varieties: 'Williams Bon Chrétien' with 'Conference' and 'Doyenné du Comice', which in any case would have been my recommendation for reliable results.

Whilst neither plums nor cherries are easy to manage as trained trees it can be done but considerable pruning expertise is required for long term success.

Soil sickness

It is always wise to avoid replanting any fruit in the same ground in which that particular fruit has just been growing. In addition to making their own particular nutritional demands on the soil each and every plant or tree exudes toxins which accumulate in a build-up around the root extremities; it is this combination of factors that results in soil sickness. So here, as in the vegetable growing area, crop rotation can eliminate problems of this kind. Whenever I am faced with a situation where there is no completely new site available, I site the replanting hole as far away as possible from where the old tree was taken out. With soft fruit I make sure that the new planting rows are between the lines of the old ones. While these answers are not ideal I have found that with liberal amounts of well-rotted compost dug in prior to planting, satisfactory results are usually obtained. Chemical soil sterilization can be an alternative and Dazomet has proved very successful, especially in the replanting of strawberries and raspberries.

Mulching

Mulching with well rotted compost is particularly useful to conserve moisture on light soils. Cane fruits always benefit from an annual dressing to keep the roots cool and moist throughout the summer but it must be well rotted otherwise a nitrogen deficiency situation develops. For all cane fruits it is far better to mulch than to dig the compost in between the rows which would risk breaking the near-surface feeding

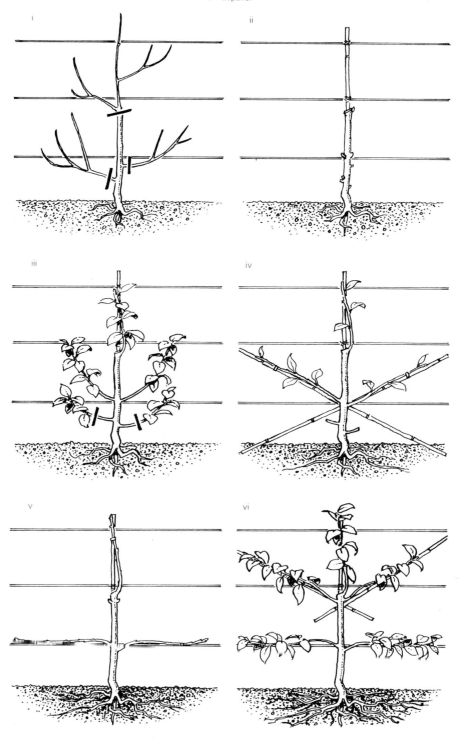

i

ii

iii

iv

v

vi

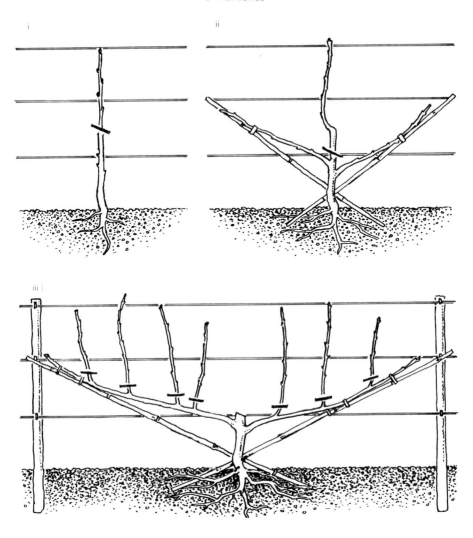

b – Fan trained

i   ii

iii

Fig. 14   Fruit trees: espalier and fan-trained.
(a) Espalier (i) First winter following planting showing places for pruning cuts on a two–three year old bush. (ii) After cuts. (iii) Growth produced in following summer. (iv) Support canes fixed in position; lowest shoots cut back. (v) Second winter. (vi) Second growing season showing second pair of support canes.
(b) Fan-trained. (i) Maiden tree cut back to 2 ft (30 cm) at end of first winter. (ii) Two side shoots are selected for training. The vertical shoot is cut when the 'training' shoots are approximately $1\frac{1}{2}$ ft (45 cm) in length. (iii) Second winter: shoots are re-tied lower and cut back to $1\frac{1}{2}$ ft (45 cm). Diagram also shows growth made in second summer and pruning cuts in third winter.

roots. A thin mulch is best but it must be thick enough to hold the moisture underneath without preventing air penetration into the soil, a mulch of this nature can effectively suppress a lot of the weeds.

Grassing down

At Clack's Farm we have experimented with apples grown in both grass and cultivated soil. Grassing down dessert apples does improve the colour but it is something that should be delayed for at least three years after planting, until the young trees have established themselves.

However, grassing down is not something I would recommend for trees on dwarfing rootstocks as it tends to slow down extension growth and cause tree weakness. When planting into grass cut out a circle at least 3 ft (0.9 m) in diameter and keep the circle weed free, otherwise the young tree will have a tottering time before it gets going.

Pollination

As all of our fruits are by nature simply vehicles for the production and distribution of seed it is absolutely essential with very few exceptions, that fertilization of the open blossom should be accomplished satisfactorily. Whilst some varieties are self-fertile most need the presence of another variety or even two varieties in open blossom at the same time. Cross-pollination, in other words the transfer of viable pollen from flower to flower may be achieved by bees or other pollinating insects and by the wind, which often plays a considerable part in the fertilization business. In every instance warmth is needed for the pollen to be viable, that is why warm sunny days at blossom time are so important.

Weed control

For soft fruits especially weed competition can be serious; weeds compete for moisture, nutrients, light and air – hence the need to start with clean ground. I have often used a cleaning crop of potatoes to get rid of couch grass, nettles or other perennial weeds. The many cultivation movements involved in growing potatoes will effectively clean the dirtiest ground in a single season. After that, starting with a clean soft fruit plot is one thing, keeping it clean afterwards is another. I still advocate the Dutch hoe as being the best tool for the job and I use it regularly.

Starting early in the season when maybe the weed seedlings have not yet emerged, that is the time to get on top of the weed problem, every white thread destroyed means an easier and better fruit season. Other advantages of using the Dutch hoe are that the soil gets aerated regularly and the soft fruit roots are not damaged.

Fruit growing in containers

Some of the finest fruit I have ever produced was grown in tubs or boxes, it was part of an exercise to demonstrate that fruit can be grown on a balcony, patio or even a backyard devoid of soil. The containers (Fig. 15) need to be large enough to house the roots. If the containers are of wooden construction it is advisable to treat the wood first with a horticulturally safe wood preservative, not creosote. Drainage holes in the bottom are essential but it is still necessary to have the container slightly raised off the ground if the holes are in the bottom, otherwise the drain-away is not effective. Many modern containers have their drainage holes in the sides just above ground level which does away with the need for raising the container.

For apples, pears and other fruits 2 ft (0.6 m) square containers with a minimum depth of 2 ft (0.6 m) are ideal; it is this sort of container that I have used for several years. Large plastic plant pots are less satisfactory as the trees tend to blow over unless supported in some way. I have used peat-based potting compost, but for trees that are going to remain in the same compost for years I prefer a soil based compost such as John Innes no. 2. From time to time it is necessary to clean the top compost up and then apply some replacement compost as a top dressing.

As regards the rest of the management, the ordinary fruit growing rules apply. In all cases the fruit trees will depend on you for water and feeding, however heavy the spring rains and showers in the summer may be – very little of it will find its way into the containers. One advantage of growing fruit in containers is that the more tender subjects such as peaches, nectarines and apricots can be moved to a greenhouse or similar shelter until you are sure that the spring frosts have finished.

Propagation

This is something I leave to the professional nurseryman. Whilst I am sure it can be fun budding or grafting or even growing your own fruit trees from seed, I doubt whether, even if successful, the ordinary gardener could justify the purchase of the rootstocks for the job. Seed of course is cheaper, in fact no cost at all but you have to remember that every seedling is an individual and it would be a million to one chance to finish up with a really good new variety.

Pruning

Pruning never has been an exact science, even the most successful commercial growers have their own ideas on the subject. I aim at

Fruit tree pruning in November – shortening the laterals, taking care to ensure that each cut is made close to a bud.

Fig. 15 (*Left*) Planting a fruit tree in a container.
(*a*) Bore three or four holes in base of oak barrel, for drainage. (*b*) Place layer of crocks in bottom of tub. (*c*) Add leaf-mould/compost to such a depth as will bring the tree to the right level when planted. (*d*) Place the tree with its root ball in position. (*e*) Add the remaining compost, firming down, especially around the sides of the tub. The final soil surface should be about 1 in (2.5 cm) below the rim to allow for watering. (*f*) Stake the plant and insert label.

keeping a tree open so that the fruit can develop with light and air around it. Snipping here and there with a pair of secateurs often results in the removal of many fruiting buds and a tree shaped like a thickly clothed ornamental.

The first pruning after planting determines the future tree shape and type, for instance a maiden tree with its single stem cut back during the winter (Fig. 16) will develop into a dwarf bush tree with a 2 ft (60 cm) stem or thereabouts. Older trees will come from the nursery with a developed branch framework; slightly shortening the branches will encourage more branches to develop. Drastic pruning at any time urges a tree to make more and still more wood growth, usually devoid of fruit buds.

From the beginning pruning should be designed to keep the centre of the tree open (Fig. 17), each pruning cut should be made carefully as the position of the bud below in relation to the cut determines the direction in which the branch from it will develop. With the exception of trained trees I prune once a year, preferably in November or as near to this time as possible.

If at all possible I avoid routine pruning on both plums and cherries, neither take kindly to it. However, sometimes it is necessary to remove crossing branches, then May is my time for the job – a clean saw cut followed by a covering of bitumen paint on the wound surface to keep out silver leaf, a nasty disease which can creep in when a branch breaks or is sawn off.

Root pruning

Prior to the widespread use of dwarfing rootstocks, periodical root pruning was often tried, as a means to restrict the development of extension growth and to induce the production of fruit buds. I have in years past tried it but never with results that would persuade me to recommend it. The need to consider root pruning is no longer important or practical, for those with old large fruit trees which are more often than not unprofitable, it is far better to replace them with varieties worked on the newer rootstocks.

Bark ringing

This is another old-fashioned method used in attempts to restrict tree growth and improve fruit production. In theory the tracks cut into the bark would slow down the flow of sap but in practice the cut bark quickly calloused over the $\frac{1}{2}$–1 in (1–3 cm) wide tracks, with the result that the tree growth rate was soon back to normal plus a serious risk of canker in the wound area.

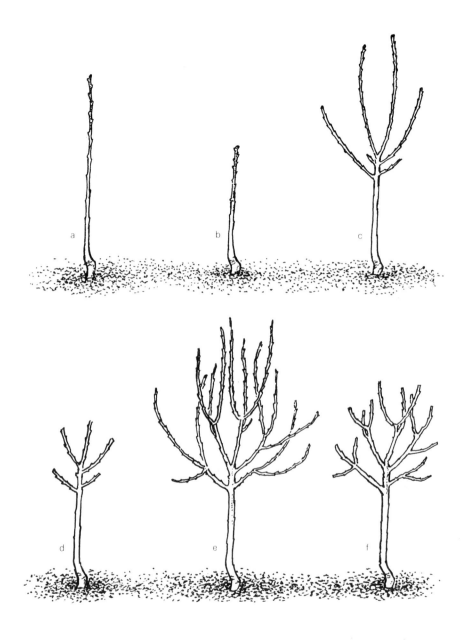

Fig. 16 Winter pruning of young trees.
(a) Newly planted 'maiden'. (b) Cut back to 60 cm (24 in). (c) The next winter
before pruning. (d) After pruning: the new shoots selected as leaders have been cut
back by two-thirds. (e) The following winter: the three-year-old tree before
pruning. (f) After pruning: the leader shoots have been cut back again by about
two-thirds.

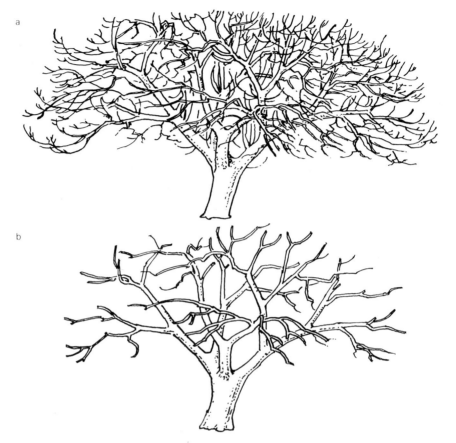

Fig. 17 Pruning: Opening up the centre of a fruit tree. (*a*) Before pruning. (*b*) After pruning.

Fertilizers

All fruit likely to stay put, crop and give a good yield for several years will need supplementary feeding with so called 'artificial' fertilizers. This word artificial can be misleading, whilst it is true that the ingredients are man made and compounded into fertilizers such as Growmore, the essential elements supplied to the plants by its use, nitrogen (N), phosphorus (P), and potassium (K) are all present naturally in most soils. Few if any of our soils have sufficient of these three essential plant nutrients to maintain permanent or semi-permanent fruit in a continuous and profitable cropping condition. As an alternative to Growmore fertilizer which, with its high potassium content is excellent for fruit generally, I would recommend PBI Back to Nature fertilizer which is largely based on organic ingredients; another entirely organic fertilizer is fish, blood and bone. Both have produced excellent results at Clack's Farm. The advantage of organic-based fertilizers is that they do also supply minute quantities of various trace elements, some of which are invaluable. I can remember a deficiency problem on the heavy Thurgarton clay which defied the efforts of the soil chemists to find a solution; our raspberries in particular were poor until we switched to a meat and bone fertilizer, the results more than justified the higher cost.

Each of the essential nutrients plays its part. Nitrogen provides the energy for growth and potassium is needed for general health. Without sufficient potassium (potash), the size, colour and sweetness are lacking in fruit and it is literally impossible to grow satisfactory crops of 'Cox's Orange Pippin' apples. At one time it was said that phosphates in any form were wasted on fruit but our work at the Lenton Research Station in Nottingham showed that there was a relationship between the levels of phosphates and the incidence of mildew, a low phosphate level resulting in an increase of apple mildew. We were also able to show that too much potassium tended to cause a magnesium deficiency with its symptoms of yellowing between the leaf veins.

For me a balanced feeding is as important as is the timing of the applications. Applied towards the end of February the nutrients are carried down by the late winter rains in time to be available when growth starts in the spring. In the case of Growmore fertilizer the rate I use is 2–3 oz per sq yd (68–102 g per sq m) in the tree-root areas or between the rows of soft fruit. Fertilizer applications later in the season are often wasted unless well watered in especially in a dry growing season.

Foliar feeding and trace element deficiencies

Products are now available for spraying on to the trees or plants during the growing season, the aim is then to get a quick response. This way of feeding can be useful in cases where fruit trees or plants are showing signs of stress midway through the growing season when it would probably be too late for soil-applied fertilizers to correct the situation. In common with organic fertilizers, most foliar feed products do help in cases of suspected trace element deficiencies of which the most common are magnesium, boron and iron. Here at Clack's Farm we have a tendency to boron deficiency and unless corrected certain apple varieties, 'Egremont Russet' in particular, suffer from bitter pit (brown skin spots with specks of brown flesh underneath). Our corrective treatment is a once in three years application of domestic borax at the rate of 1 oz per 30 sq yd (30 g per 25 sq m).

To avoid over application and this is important as borax in excess assumes the role of plant killer, I apply the borax in solution using an ordinary watering can fitted with a rose. Whilst I appreciate that it is generally understood that liming the ground for fruit is not advisable except on very exceptional soils, perhaps I should emphasize this point as liming is liable to induce manganese, boron and iron deficiencies on otherwise good fruit land and bring with it all sorts of unnecessary problems. Being too heavy handed with potassium fertilizers can result in a magnesium deficiency (yellowing between the green veins of the leaves). Whether or not this deficiency is natural or induced, my corrective treatment is commercial Epsom salts (magnesium sulphate) applied at the rate of 2 oz per sq yd (68 g per sq m).

Fruit quality

Nothing but the best satisfies me; not only must each variety have good flavour qualities and if possible be coupled with good cropping ability but, when ripe and ready for picking, it must look good and above all taste good. The effect of climate, soil types and nutrition have already been discussed; next comes the question of variety.

When planting soft fruit a wrong choice is not too serious; it can be corrected within a couple of years but nevertheless it is a waste of time and effort. However, in the case of tree fruits one is undertaking a much longer term project. One may have to wait two or three years before you can even get a taste of the apples or pears, and by the time the trees come into full bearing it is often too late in one's life to consider correcting the mistake. Flavour is an essential quality and unless it is naturally present in a variety no cultural or fertilizer treatments will put it there. Commercially popular varieties are not necessarily the right choice for garden culture where flavour will or should be far more important than the shelf life and profit. Crop yield is of course important and local knowledge can be valuable as the performance of varieties vary tremendously from district to district. Freshness is a unique quality in home grown fruit – what could be better than a dish of your own strawberries or raspberries fully ripened with the sun's warmth still in them and a jug of cream at hand?

Fruit storage

Here again it is largely a question of variety and generally speaking only the late maturing apples keep in good condition for any length of time. The varieties we store for dessert are 'Cox's Orange Pippin', 'Idared' and 'Golden Delicious'. Our Cox's usually keep us well supplied until Christmas then after that and until March or even early

April we rely on Golden Delicious, a much maligned variety only because it is usually picked on the continent before it is mature and has not acquired its flavour. 'Idared' is our March/April dual-purpose apple, good as a dessert and for our apple pies.

Apples must be fully mature at the time of picking otherwise they will quickly shrivel and certainly lose their flavour. To test for maturity we lift the fruit gently upwards, then if the stalk parts from the branch without the need for even a gentle pull it is ready. Here at Clack's Farm it is usually the end of October before we pick Cox's and often not till the first week in November before 'Golden Delicious' and 'Idared' are ready to be put in store.

Pears are different; even the best keepers have a relatively short storage life and need watching almost daily, otherwise internal rotting sets in. Unlike apples we pick our pears slightly before maturity. We never allow them to ripen on the trees otherwise the flesh is gritty and dry instead of luscious and juicy. Fruit picking for storage should not be rushed, careful handling is essential, the slightest bruising resulting in early rotting. We always segregate damaged fruit, bird pecked or pest attacked, for immediate use as only perfect specimens keep well. Whilst length of storage depends basically on variety, storage conditions are also always important. We are fortunate in having a cool, brick built outbuilding where the temperature variations are limited; as an ordinary store it is ideal. Very dry or warm storage conditions are unsuitable so centrally heated rooms are out. A large box with ventilation holes in an outhouse could be a substitute for a fruit room.

In every case the fruit should be picked dry and allowed time to cool down before storage. We store our fruit without wrapping in slatted trays in single layers but this does not mean that wrapping each apple or pear separately does not have advantages (Fig. 18). Special oiled paper wraps are available for the job but ordinary newspaper used in the same way does isolate rotting to the individual specimen. Long-term storage of soft fruit is easy, especially when it can be picked ripe and in good condition on a dry day; ours goes into the freezer with the minimum delay. Contrary to some ideas put forward we find that it is well worth while freezing strawberries. They may lose their firmness but not their flavour, we use them in several ways: for a fruit salad they are defrosted mixed with the other fruit so all the juice and flavour is preserved, or they may be half defrosted and have hot custard poured over them. A third way is to liquidize them while half frozen and make a strawberry mousse.

We also use the freezer approach for storing damsons, plums, peeled and prepared apples and pears; we are never without apple sauce

Fig. 18 Storing apples.
(*a*) The most efficient way storing apples is to individually wrap them and then to place them in single layers in wooden trays. (*b*) Store the filled trays in a cool outbuilding or shed, not in the warmth indoors.

stored frozen in handy half pint cartons. Instead of buying tinned pears we freeze our surplus 'William Bon Cretien' and 'Clapp's Favourite' pears lightly cooked in 50% syrup. In our opinion no canned pears can compare with them. Cooking apple varieties tend to freeze better than the dessert ones which tend to go soft; uncooked pears with us have been a disappointment as they lose their firmness.

My favourite fruit

Dessert apples
As a youngster in Cambridgeshire with my parents' large orchard close at hand and easy to raid, I quickly discovered which of the apples appealed to my taste. A standard 'Cox's Orange Pippin' tree which stood just inside the gate was my favourite, the fruits were more often than not small but when fully ripe the flesh was firm and full to brimming over with juice and flavour. Cox's still remain my favourite although I have never enjoyed them quite as much as when I picked the apples off that old tree which no doubt was growing on its own roots. Its season, i.e. the time that the fruit is at its best for consumption, is November/January (mid-season flowering). Another dessert variety of boyhood memories is 'Blenheim Orange'; I remember when

each October I used to climb the large trees at home and enjoy its unique flavour. It still remains one of the best keeping apples but worked on modern rootstocks it has lost some of its flavour appeal for me. A point to remember is that 'Blenheim Orange' is self-sterile and needs two pollinators blossoming at the same time. Season November/January (mid-season flowering).

For small gardens 'Charles Ross' is a most reliable cropper. The fruit often tends to be on the large side, it is an attractive apple, round pale yellow with red stripes in its flushed skin. I appreciate it most when it is just becoming fully ripe, later on it tends to become woolly fleshed. Nevertheless it is a good garden apple, especially if the soil is inclined to be chalky; a condition which does not suit all varieties. Season October/November (mid-season flowering).

For an August apple my choice is 'Discovery'. It is difficult to believe the report that it is a seedling from 'Worcester Pearmain' as it is so sweet, full of juice with a flavour not unlike that of 'Cox's Orange Pippin'. The fruit is round and flattish with the most attractive yellow to bright red colourings. Be careful when you prune it as it is a tip bearer. Season mid-August/September (mid-season flowering). We regard it as one of the best pollinators for 'Cox's Orange Pippin'.

As a consistent cropper 'Egremont Russet' lives up to its reputation, with us it is a good garden apple with the true russet flavour, provided its nutrient needs are cared for otherwise it can suffer from cracking and bitter pit. On our soil 1 oz (30 g) of domestic borax to 30 sq yd (25 sq m) has solved the problem; we repeat the treatment every third year. Season October/December (early flowering).

'Epicure' an early apple with a unique aromatic flavour appeals to me, on its day when it is fully ripe it is truly delicious, so sweet and full of luscious juice. It is a medium-sized, flattish apple with a greenish-yellow skin flushed with red; we find that it is inclined to set too many fruits which usually makes it necessary for us to do some early thinning. Season September (mid-season flowering).

'Fortune' is an apple that seems to be somewhat particular about the soil type and district, here it does well without suffering from cracking. A great apple and a regular cropper, it is another 'Laxton' raised apple with an aromatic flavour, medium sized with an attractive skin, yellow with red streaks. Season September/October (mid-season flowering).

'Golden Delicious' if you grow it yourself as we do is a good apple – forget the idea that it is insipid. Commercially grown in France and mass marketed here whilst still immature has given it a bad name for quality. At Clack's Farm it is our most consistent cropper; with more warmth it would have a clearer skin complexion but gathered fully mature in early November we love it both for eating straight away or for storing until March, after that it still keeps but tends to lose its flavour. Season November/March (late flowering).

The easiest apple to grow in a small garden is 'James Grieve'. It has never let us down but it must be picked ripe and eaten straight from the tree, I have always enjoyed its delicious flavour and very juicy flesh. It is not a keeper, due no doubt to the tenderness of its yellow flesh, we handle it very gently to prevent bruising. Season September/early October (flowering mid-season).

An apple with a checkered career is 'Lord Lambourne'. Years ago it was bedevilled with a virus which resulted in weak branches, so called 'rubbery wood'. Now it is possible to purchase virus-free trees and it can once again be a useful mid-season dessert apple for a small garden. The flesh is solid and crisp with a super Cox-like flavour. It is a flattish apple, never highly coloured and the skin varies from a yellowish green to a yellowish red. 'Lord Lambourne' is by nature less vigorous than most, so for a dwarf bush tree I would plant it on MM 106 rootstock rather than Malling 9 rootstock. Season October/November (early flowering).

'Red Ellison', a sport from an old time favourite 'Ellison's Orange Pippin', is equal in all respects to its parent including its resistance to spring-frost blossom damage. In spite of its tendency to be a biennial cropper for me it is a must, there is nothing to equal its aromatic aniseed-like flavour. In common with 'Cox's Orange Pippin', for large and good coloured fruit it needs adequate potassium in the soil. Season September/October (late flowering).

A variety for those who are unable to grow 'Cox's Orange Pippin' is 'Sunset'; it is a smaller apple with firmer flesh and usually needs early thinning to get good sized fruits. I always grew it in Nottinghamshire where the seasons are often on the cool side. Season November/December (mid-season flowering).

'Worcester Pearmain' is an apple I still grow and enjoy, simply because I can pick it ripe from the tree and eat it straightaway. Off the tree it soon loses its flavour and the flesh goes woolly. Its real value here is as a pollinator for other late flowering varieties. Season late August/early September (late flowering).

Apart from the list of my favourite dessert apples for which the criterion has been the appeal to my palate, it would be wrong not to mention a few other varieties:

'Charles Ross' for instance is a reliable cropper, the apples tend to be very large with most attractive colourings, pale yellow with red stripes to flush its cheeks. Plant it on MM 106 rootstock and it will succeed on a chalky soil. Season October/December (mid-season flowering).

As a very late keeper 'Crispin' would be a good choice. It is a large version of 'Golden Delicious' (one of its parents). Originally it was named 'Mustu' by its Japanese raisers. Grown here the skin has a muddy look, the flesh lacks flavour but whilst classed as a dessert variety it cooks well and then the taste is quite good. Season December/April (mid-season flowering).

'Idared' is another dessert variety in the long-keeping, dual purpose category; it is one of our freest croppers. The apples are medium sized with an attractive skin; after storage it tends to lose its dessert flavour but its cooking qualities remain. My main complaint against it is its susceptibility to apple mildew – routine control spraying is essential. Season November/April (early flowering).

Perhaps I should mention 'Superb', at one time known as 'Laxton's Superb', often planted because it looks so good as a young tree at the point of purchase, however its whippy growth habit and biennial cropping is against it as a variety for the small garden. Perhaps I am prejudiced but I have not planted it at Clack's Farm. Season November/February (mid-season flowering).

Culinary apples

Now for my favourite culinary varieties. Of course the finest late keeping apple is 'Bramley's Seedling'. Unfortunately it is not one of the easiest varieties to grow, in addition the blossom buds and open blossom are susceptible to frost damage. Another problem in a small garden is its vigorous growth habit but this can be controlled by planting it on Malling 9 or Malling 26 rootstock and growing it either as a dwarf bush or cordon, providing of course that you remember when pruning that it is a tip bearer. As it is a triploid, two suitable pollinators nearby are needed; here we tried 'Discovery' and 'Early Victoria' with complete success. 'Bramley' is a large green apple ready for picking towards the end of October or early November for storing. Season November/March (mid-season flowering).

'Lane's Prince Albert' with its large greenish-yellow apples with red streaks is a reliable alternative to 'Bramley's Seedling', it is a good consistent cropper. The fruit cooks well, is soft with excellent flavour. For the small garden it is an excellent choice although the tree has a spreading habit. Season November/March (late season flowering).

Now for the early cooker, here my favourite is 'Early Victoria'; it is a tremendous cropper. It starts our season as the thinnings are ready by the middle of July, from then on until the end of August it is picked as needed for the kitchen. Unfortunately 'Early Victoria' does tend to be a biennial cropper but early thinning does help to prevent it. The apples are medium sized, conical with yellowish-green skin, the flesh cooks soft and the flavour is superb. Season July/August (mid-season flowering).

A slightly later apple 'Grenadier' is a more consistent cropper with individual fruits larger and more irregular in shape than 'Early Victoria'. Again the skin is yellowish-green, the flesh cooks frothy but the flavour is not as good. Tree vigour is such that in a small garden I would always plant it on a dwarfing rootstock such as Malling 9 or Malling 26. Season August/September (mid-season flowering).

The cooking apple we almost worship on account of its supreme flavour is the 'Rev. W. Wilks'. In my opinion it is without equal for baking or cooking in any form. It is a large apple with a creamy white skin and on occasion with slight flushing, the flesh is white and soft; it cooks frothy. Baked with the core removed, filled with brown sugar and sultanas it becomes a feast to be remembered. We grow it on Malling 9 rootstock as a dwarf bush tree. As with all good things there are snags – it is a truly biennial bearer, but we have overcome by planting two trees one of which we de-blossomed once to establish a rhythm, giving us each season one tree full of beautiful apples. We have to thin early to get the benefit of the large baked-apple potential. Season September/October (early season flowering).

Another slightly later, large cooking apple is 'Lord Derby', a variety to plant in any garden subject to spring frost damage, unlike most other varieties it will set its fruit without the seed being formed. The apples have a greenish-yellow skin, the flesh is white, firm and somewhat acid, it cooks well and has good flavour. It is an upright vigorous grower; with us on Malling 9 rootstock grown as a dwarf bush it is a regular cropper. Season October/November (late season flowering).

Apart from my favourite cookers I must mention 'Newton Wonder', in spite of it being a biennial cropper it is an excellent keeper. As a boy this largish yellow apple with a red flush and stripes meant more to me as an eater in the winter than a cooker. Alas we no longer grow it on account of its vigorous, spreading growth habit. Season November/March (late season flowering).

Pears
The one thing to remember is that pears appreciate warmth and dislike wind, hence the reason why they do best in our south-eastern counties. Always wait until pears are mature before picking then ripen them off the tree, otherwise the flesh may be gritty.

The garden pear that is undoubtedly regarded as the number one is 'Conference'. There are superior varieties but 'Conference' is one of the easiest to grow and its flesh and flavour qualities are very acceptable. For the small garden it is the most reliable cropper, it is fairly vigorous and it can succeed if need be on its own without a pollinator. Medium-sized fruit with a longish neck and dark russeted skin is characteristic of the variety. When fully ripe a conference pear is full of very sweet juice. Season October/November (mid-season flowering).

'Doyenné du Comice' must be my favourite but it is one of the most difficult to grow. Here at Clack's Farm it does fairly well grown as a cordon. It is no use planting it on its own as it needs at least two good pollinators planted nearby. Well grown and favoured with a good summer the fruit is large with a pale yellow, russeted skin; if only we had a kinder climate, more warmth and less wind. Season November (late season flowering).

'Beurre Hardy', one of our pollinators for 'Doyenné-du Comice', is inclined to be a vigorous grower. However, it is a reliable cropper although the fruit may be uneven in shape. The greenish-yellow skin is covered with russeted patches flushed with a trace of red. On its peak day the flesh is tender, juicy and full of flavour. Season October (mid to late season flowering).

The ever popular 'Louise Bonne de Jersey' makes an upright tree, ideal for small gardens. It is a regular cropper, especially when planted, as it is here, near a suitable pollinator such as 'Conference'. When fully ripe its medium sized fruits with their yellowish-green skins flushed with red are very tempting, then the juicy flesh is tender with an excellent flavour. Season October (early to mid-season flowering).

'Glou Morceau', our second pollinator for 'Doyenné du Comice' shares with it an appreciation for a warm climate. A great pity for the northern gardeners as it is a late pear with a truly delicious flavour. Season December/January (late flowering).

'Onward', one of our more recent additions, has excellent flavour, not surprising as 'Doyenné du Comice' is one of its parents, we are growing it as a cordon and are quite pleased with its three-year cropping record. Season September (late flowering).

Last but not least amongst my favourites is 'Williams Bon Chrétien', the most widely grown pear in the world; under its other name 'Bartlett' you find it on shop shelves in tins. It must be picked before the fruit turns yellow otherwise the flesh is lacking in juice and flavour. It is a medium sized pear, a vigorous grower and free cropper. Gathered mature, stored in a shoe box and checked daily for ripeness, that's the way to enjoy the luscious juice and excellent flavour. Better still, if you can, store the fruit in a 'pocket' in a stack of new mown hay. Always a great pear on its day, after that it soon goes bad. Season September (mid-season flowering).

There are many other varieties, some good some not so good, the favourites listed here have been selected for quality and with the exception of 'Doyenné du Comice' all are consistent croppers, subject to efficient pollination.

When in 1956 we bought Clack's Farm we inherited some old trees of 'Clapp's Favourite' pears. After some tree surgery they do now on occasion crop heavily but they are too large for effective spraying. We have without success tried planting maiden trees of this variety but have come to the conclusion that it needs to be double worked on its rootstock. We intend to have another go simply because it is a real winner when frozen in syrup. Season August (late season flowering).

Plums

Plums are very hardy and provided the land is well drained they will thrive. However, on light soils they will need water during the summer to prevent the fruit from shrivelling. Periodic applications of garden lime are advisable except on naturally calcareous soil types. From years of experience I would always recommend clean cultivation under the trees as plums never do as well when their root areas are covered with either weeds or grass. As mentioned previously free standing plum trees do not appreciate pruning. On account of bullfinches every year systematically stripping our trees of their swelling fruit buds we have switched over to growing some varieties fan trained on a fence. However, this is beset with problems; the pruning has to be done very carefully otherwise we get a lot of wood growth and little fruit bud. In common with free standing plum trees these trained trees tend to make more strong wood growth in the first two or three years after planting, after that we find that they do ultimately settle down to less wood growth and more fruit buds.

Once a plum tree has settled down into fruiting we give it an annual Growmore fertilizer application towards the end of February and on our slightly acid soil an application of garden lime every other year is needed to make sure that the critical stone forming is accomplished successfully, a wise precaution on any soil except the chalky types.

Silver leaf is a killer, the fungus develops within the wood, the silvery appearance of the leaves is just one symptom, dark brown or black stains in the cut branches another. The silver leaf Order of 1923 requires the removal and burning of infected dead wood before the

15th July; infected dead wood or tree stumps produce fungus fructifi-
cations which, with the aid of the wind, spread the disease far and
wide.

Varieties. Top of the list for an early stewing plum is 'Rivers Early
Prolific'; from childhood to this very day I look forward to July when
these smallish blue plums are ready. There is no need to wait until they
are soft, they cook well, the flavour is good and the juice is luscious.
Season July (early season flowering).

For the first dessert plum 'Greengage' is my choice but it must be
the true gage, no other has its flavour, nor its unfortunate and unpre-
dictable cropping habits. It is far from being a reliable cropper and
must have a late flowering pollinator mate, give it that and you discover a joy of a new dimension in plums. When ripe the fruits are olive
green with a slight red flush and spots, as I write my mouth waters.
Season late August (late season flowering).

It would be impossible not to include 'Victoria', the most popular
plum although its dessert flavour is only moderate, the flesh is sweet.
Well grown, thinned early it can make a large plum and as the size
increases so does its flavour and quality generally, stewed it is excellent
so it is a truly dual purpose plum. For the gardener who can only plant
a single plum tree it is the right variety as it is self-fertile but like all
self-fertile trees it crops better if there is another variety nearby which
flowers at the same time. When fully ripe the plums turn bright red
with some darker spots. Season August/September (mid-season
flowering).

If you have to settle for a more reliable cropper with a gage flavour
the choice must be 'Cambridge Gage', like most gages its fruits are not
large. However, when ripe the yellowish-green skins are full of well
flavoured juicy flesh. Season August/September (late season
flowering).

Now for a tip-top quality dessert plum, 'Kirke's Blue', a variety best
suited to the warmer climate areas. When fully ripe the medium to
large plums are purple skinned with an overall blue bloom, inside the
flesh is juicy and the flavour superb. I am delighted to be growing it
again, this time as a free standing tree sheltered by a six foot (1.8 m)
fence from the north and the east winds. Season September (mid-
season flowering).

'Jefferson's Gage' is a good cropper, its large ripe fruits are golden,
slightly flushed and spotted with red russeted patches. The flesh is
juicy, sweet and has excellent flavour. Season September (early season
flowering).

We find our favourite damsons in the hedgerows round Clack's Farm, the variety 'Shropshire Damson'. It is the true small blue damson far superior to the 'Merryweather' damson which is really a medium sized plum completely lacking the damson flavour. The 'Shropshire Damson' makes a small tree, being self-fertile. It usually crops freely after taking three or four years to settle down. Season September/October (late season flowering).

Raspberries
With wild raspberries happy and healthy in the west of Scotland we have a clear indication of the soil and climatic conditions they need. Give them a well drained soil that is never short of moisture in a district where the summers are cool, then the rest is easy. On light soils the addition of organic matter to improve the moisture-holding capacity is a must, well-rotted compost or peat pre-planting will do the job. Afterwards an annual mulching with compost on any type of soil does three jobs, it helps the soil to retain its moisture, it keeps the roots cool, and, as it breaks down, supplies valuable nutrients.

Before planting I make sure that the ground is free from perennial weeds and that it has been dug over to the full depth of a new spade. Whilst raspberries will tolerate partial shade they crop best in a full sun position. It is wise to start with healthy young canes carrying a Ministry of Agriculture Certificate of Health. On no account plant canes lifted from a fruiting row, which more likely than not will be virus infected. The effect of virus in raspberries is progressive, as it develops plant health and crop yields deteriorate slowly but surely. I maintain a replanting programme and work on the assumption that starting with healthy canes I can expect to crop them for ten seasons before a reducing crop yield makes replacement advisable.

My planting time is November so that by early spring the young canes 18 in (45 cm) apart in the row have made plenty of new roots (Fig. 19). March is the time when I cut down the newly planted canes to 6 in (15 cm). This means that summer fruiting varieties do not fruit that season, their first task is to get well established and grow sturdy canes for the following year but we do allow the autumn fruiting varieties to crop in the following September or October.

The main difference between summer and autumn fruiting varieties is that immediately after fruiting the old canes of the summer fruiting varieties are cut out and the strongest of the new growth tied in for cropping the following season, whereas autumn fruiting raspberry canes are always completely cut down early in March each year, they then fruit on the current season's growth.

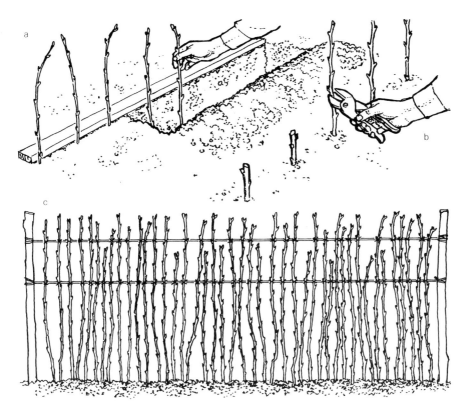

Fig. 19 Raspberries.
(*a*) Planting out the new canes in the autumn. (*b*) Canes cut back to 4 in (12 cm) above the ground in the following March. (*c*) Mature canes tied in to wires, which themselves are supported by wooden or metal posts.

We use posts and three strands of wires for supporting the canes, I like the top wire 5 ft (1.5 m) from the ground and the other two spaced 18 in (45 cm) apart.

Varieties. We have yet to find a better flavoured raspberry than 'Malling Jewel'; it is a good cropper with its berries well clear of the foliage and thus easy to pick. A related variety 'Malling Promise' may be a heavier cropper but its berries are slightly softer, the flavour is good but not equal to 'Malling Jewel'.

Why only two varieties? We have tried others such as 'Delight' and 'Malling Admiral', both are vigorous growers with large berries, ideal for the show bench but with little or no flavour. 'Glen Clova' is another flavourless one which is very subject to virus disease and should always be grown on its own.

For autumn fruiting varieties again we have two outstanding varieties: 'September' and 'Zeva'. The latter produces the larger berries but they are softer than 'September' and in a wet autumn the berries on 'September' are far less likely to go down with mildew – both have a true raspberry flavour. By September our blackbirds are only interested in the fruits of the hedgerows and we have never found it necessary to net any of our autumn fruiting varieties.

Strawberries

We aim at planting out new strawberry beds in August or at the latest September, then in the well-prepared, clean, weed-free ground the plants are settled down by spring with strong root systems and crowns full of flower buds ready to crop in their first season. The secret of success is to have a liberal amount of well-rotted compost or manure down underneath the plants. As with raspberries they should be obtained from stock covered by a Ministry of Agriculture health certificate. To buy or accept job lots is false economy, starting with virus infected plants can only result in disappointments.

We do have some sloping ground so we are able to plant our strawberries on higher ground in a sunny position, this helps to minimize spring frost damage to the blossom and at the same time gives the plants the best cropping conditions. A feed with PBI Back to Nature fertilizer in March is our annual feeding routine.

Summer fruiting varieties. There is still no argument as far as I am concerned, 'Royal Sovereign' is the finest flavoured strawberry. If only it had some degree of resistance to virus diseases it would always be our first choice. We go on growing it only to be disappointed time and again. The most reliable variety is 'Cambridge Favourite', it has vigour and is a heavy cropper but its flavour is moderate. 'Tamella' is a winner, good cropper and above average flavour, we use it particularly for forcing in 5 in or 6 in (13 or 15 cm) pots so that we can have strawberries and cream as a special treat early in May. To follow 'Tamella' we grow 'Domanil' and 'Tenira' outside, they ripen a little later but are good croppers with real strawberry flavour.

Autumn fruiting varieties. In our experience a wet summer followed by a dry warm September and October is needed for a really good crop of clean, colourful and well flavoured autumn strawberries but, given that, both 'Rabunda' and 'Gento' continue to justify a place. 'Rabunda' is the heaviest cropper and more vigorous grower, whilst 'Gento' has the better flavour. The berries on both are susceptible to botrytis in a cold and wet autumn; we find Boots systemic fungicide an excellent preventative spray.

What about other fruits? The remaining favourites for me are red currants, 'Red Lake' for making red currant jelly: home made it is unbeatable with roast lamb. Red currants differ from black currants in so far that they fruit on the old wood consequently there is no after fruiting pruning, if and when our bushes get over crowded I remove a few individual central branches during the winter.

Neither Riet nor I are fond of black currants, nevertheless we have a few bushes in order that we may oblige friends. For them we grow 'Boskoop Giant' for the early crop and 'Wellington XXX' to follow on. By making sure that they have a liberal Growmore fertilizer application towards the end of February and that most of the old wood is removed immediately after fruiting, we continue to get consistently good fruit yields and at the same time maintain the health of the bushes.

We grow three varieties of gooseberries, 'Careless' a variety only suitable for making pies, 'Whinham's Industry' the one with the dark red skin, full of marvellous flavour when picked fully ripe and eaten as a dessert, plus 'Leveller' another dessert variety the thinnings of which can be used for cooking.

Both gooseberries and red currants can be grown as cordons as well as bushes but black currants are only suitable for growing as bushes.

The various varieties I have mentioned have all been thoroughly tried out at Clack's Farm, they are proved croppers and above all have an abundance of flavour in their fruit. If you do plant any of them, do not make the common mistake of crowding them too closely together, do give them a chance to prove their worth in your garden.

FIVE

My favourite flowers

Instead of preparing a catalogue of plants I will take you into Clack's Farm garden, not just on one particular day but we will stay in it throughout the whole year as it is planted and maintained in such a way that there is never a day without something being in bloom. However, no plant finds a place or keeps it for long unless it has some charm which appeals to us. One of the great joys of having your own garden is that you can plant to please yourself, consequently as the season progresses any garden, and ours is no exception, reflects its owner's own ideas.

I am still influenced by the fact that at the age of about six, after long deliberation and the handling of many colourful packets of seed in a local shop, I invested my Saturday penny in a packet of mixed pansy seed. It was a miracle that the seed ever germinated in its wooden Cadbury's Milk Chocolate box perched high up on a stack of bricks in the farmyard, it must have been a risk every time I clambered up to investigate its progress. Now after decades I am still in love with pansies, I often wonder how empty my whole life might have been but for that decision as a child to buy a packet of pansy seed which gave me my first glimpse of nature's wonderland.

So it can be no surprise that pansies are always to be found in Clack's Farm garden and it would be a rare occasion if some were not found in bloom even in the depth of winter. Pansies, with their faces always turned towards the sun, reflect the glories of nature, memories of the past and the hopes of the future, as I look into each face it silently transmits peace and serenity.

However, since those days of long ago the plant breeders have improved pansies almost beyond recognition and many now are either F_1 or F_2 hybrids such as 'Golden Crown', 'Imperial Orange Prince', 'Majestic Giants', all with beautiful large faces in many colours. I must not forget 'Azure Blue'; it flowers all the year round and its self-sown seedlings come almost true to colour and size. Then there are 'Tiara' and 'Premier' mixed, two good ones for early flowering. In addition I grow a collection of the 'Swiss Giants', 'Alpenglow', 'Coronation Gold', 'Rheingold', 'Silverbride', 'Ullswater', to name but a few. I sow the seed in June in shallow drills for planting out in the autumn.

Providing we plant on ground that has had a couple of years rest from pansies all is well. To plant on the same spot year after year is asking for trouble and sooner or later pansy wilt will creep in. Incidentally aphids (greenfly) have a great affection for pansies so we spray ours regularly with a systemic insecticide.

January

Let us walk into the garden (Fig. 20) in January, a time when the groups of *Erica carnea* 'Springwood White' and 'Springwood Pink' are in full flower. These are two of the easiest heathers to grow, they ask for little except an occasional peat top dressing and for a trim when the flowering season is over. In a warm, dry, narrow south-facing border in front of the house we find *Iris unguicularis (I. stylosa)* with its mass of narrow leaves supporting the stems of the delicate lilac blue flowers; here is an example of siting success, it is a native of Algeria and thrives in sunshine and poor soil, neither does it mind being dry.

At this time the hellebores are also putting on a brave show, in spite of the fact that some of them never see the sun, in fact all do best in semi-shade. *Helleborus niger* (Christmas rose) we used to cover with cloches for early flowers, but stopped this practice because the slugs liked the cover and left us with damaged flowers. Now, without covering, it provides us with gorgeous, large, unblemished blooms, albeit somewhat later.

February

Coming into February we find not only *Helleborus foetidus* with its large clusters of pale citron bells, edged maroon but also *Helleborus orientalis* (Lenten rose), with its many delicate colours; the plants stand with their buds and wide open flowers nodding in the wind. We have a very vigorous dark purple variety, given to us by Sheila Mc-Queen, which we believe to be *Helleborous purpurascens*; it is one to make a flower arranger's dream come true.

For me the flower of the month is the snowdrop, it ignores the cold and comes to tell us that spring is not too far away. My favourite variety is 'S. Arnott', I simply adore its long stems and delicate flowers. I started with six bulbs given to me by Jack Matthews and we now have hundreds as it has multiplied so freely. The best time to lift and divide snowdrops is just after flowering whilst the foliage is still green.

Our few species crocuses flower early to keep the snowdrops company and to cheer us up with a variation in colour. It has not been easy to protect their foliage after flowering and it is so necessary for it to die

Fig. 20   Plan of the ornamental garden, 1982.

Key to plan:
1 *Prunus* 'Ukon' (Japanese flowering cherry)
2 *Sequoia sempervirens* (Californian redwood)
3 *Malus* 'Wisley' (flowering crab)
4 Pigeon loft (over); hound kennel (under)
5 Dutch barn
6 Garage
7 House
8 Farm buildings
9 Pigsties (disused)
10 16th century byre
11 Entrance and drive
12 Beech hedge
13 *Prunus* 'Fugenzo' (Japanese flowering cherry)
14 *Malus robusta* (Siberian crab)
15 *Betula pendula* 'Dalecarlica' (Swedish birch)
16 *Cedrus atlantica* 'Glauca' (blue cedar)
17 Pool and rock garden
18 *Magnolia* × *soulangiana* 'Alba Superba'
19 Peat Garden
20 *Catalpa bignonioides* (Indian bean tree)
21 Hazel nut tree
22 *Sorbus discolor* (mountain ash or rowan)
23 *Pyrus salicifolia* 'Pendula' (willow leaved pear) weeping form
24 *Laburnum* 'Vossii'
25 Fruit and vegetable garden
26 Lawn
27 *Betula pendula* 'Youngii' (Young's weeping birch)
28 Alpine Garden
29 *Kolkwitzia amabilis rosea*
30 *Prunus avium* 'Plena' (flowering cherry)
31 Rock garden plants
32 *Liriodendron tulipifera* (tulip tree)
33 Camellias
34 *Malus floribunda* (flowering crab)
35 *Malus* 'Golden Hornet' (flowering crab)
36 *Salix babylionica*
37 *Populus candicans* 'Aurora' (a variegated poplar)
38 Box hedge
39 Tea garden
40 Pump

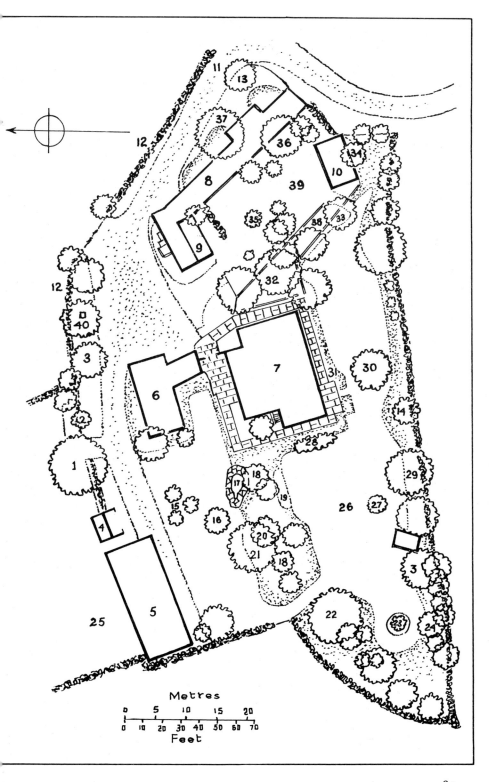

Metres

0 ... 5 ... 10 ... 15 ... 20

0 10 20 30 40 50 60 70

Feet

down naturally otherwise the bulbs are deprived of their food-store manufacturing ability. When this happens the crocuses gradually die out; the same is true for daffodils, at least that is my experience.

Gradually this month we have more colour contributors, the *Muscari* (grape hyacinth) arrive with their legions of miniature blue blooms and their desire to multiply. We have to keep them on a tight rein otherwise they take over, producing more foliage and less flowers as the years go by. Lifting and replanting the larger bulbs each autumn is the answer. What a joy it is when towards the end of the month *Iris reticulata* suddenly breaks into bloom, each flower on its own short stem a perfect purple iris. Cared for by safeguarding it against weeds it will come up smiling year after year.

March

The hybrid crocuses, those with the larger flowers in various colours, come into bloom about the same time early in March. When the sun opens the flowers, the honeybees are buzzing with activity collecting pollen for their brood. There was a time when we fed the birds during the winter in the garden. We were trying to be kind but they became the owners, the garden became their feeding territory and we were never able to enjoy our yellow crocuses, primroses, etc. So we dispensed with the bird table and artificially feeding the birds. Everybody is happy again, the birds are back working for a living in their own habitat and we enjoy their company without having to endure their destructiveness.

Chionodoxa (glory of the snow) turns up in the most unexpected places. We started with just a few bulbs in the rock garden, now each late February their exquisite and dainty flowers often greet us singly at almost every turn, perhaps we have to thank the birds for distributing their seed. Our *Eranthis* (winter aconite) struggles to survive. The truth is I am too tidy for their liking; they are at their best under a large old beech tree where weed competition is almost nil, and we have no such area. I have tried to remember not to disturb them but weeds do intervene and many of the sleeping aconites are lost, sad because a carpet of winter aconites is a great feast to the eyes wherever it occurs.

By the time we are well into March, the numbers of flowering plants increase rapidly, the little dark blue scillas, the early tulip species and the early hyacinths are in bloom. For several years now we have popped the forced Christmas hyacinths into the borders. It takes the bulbs a season to recover but that they do; we give them a little bonemeal at planting time to help them and from the second year onwards they are happy to be outside. As a matter of fact I prefer to see

The small water garden, dwarfed by the height of the wild yellow iris, from the Isle of Mull.

Above: In the new rose garden with some of the forty-six varieties; the author admires the qualities of 'Trumpeter', a delightful, free-flowering, red floribunda.

Left: Small group of *Cyclamen neapolitanum* recently established in the shelter of a rock in the alpine garden. (Even a handfork is forbidden here lest young seedlings should be disturbed.)

them flowering naturally. I could say the same about daffodils of which we have some thirty varieties planted in groups towards the back of the borders where the foliage left to die down naturally is not too unsightly. We start with 'Magnificent', a true golden trumpet variety, close by it is 'Ice Follies' which for me is top of the pops. Of course we also have 'Golden Harvest' with its large trumpets and many more. Towards the end of the daffodil season 'Cheerfulness', white and yellow, with its three or more flowers to each stem lives up to its name. Once the foliage is completely dead we clear it away, apply some super phosphate of lime at the rate of 2–3 oz per sq yd (68–102 g per sq m) and rake it in. The raking fills in the holes left by the dead foliage and so does much to thwart the narcissus fly laying its eggs close by the bulbs. Viable eggs develop into maggots that feed on the centres of the bulbs producing blindness the following season.

Darwin and May flowering tulips are too formal for our garden but we do find a place for some of the tulip species which can be left after flowering and will come up year after year. One that has given us a lot of pleasure recently is 'Red Riding Hood', its streaked foliage adding to the beauty of the bright scarlet flowers.

Primroses and polyanthus

Now that we have agreed with the birds on what is theirs and what is our territory we raise our primroses and polyanthus with confidence; sowing the seed in June I find it best to germinate it in the greenhouse using a peat based sowing compost. Too high a temperature inhibits germination so under the bench is the best place. When the seedlings are large enough to handle I prick them out, 28 to a standard-size seedtray, this time into a potting compost. The next move is outside where they wait until the autumn for the final planting out into their flowering positions. As I write in late April our F_1 'Serenade' mixed primroses are making an unbelievable display for number of blooms per plant and variety of colour. I have not seen anything to equal it in primroses and what is so good about them is that they go on to be just as vigorous in the second season. All we have to do is spray them occasionally during the summer with malathion to keep the red spider at bay. We have tried many strains of polyanthus, some seemingly have too long stems to hold up the flower heads, so we have switched over to the F_1 Pacific strain. From a packet of mixed seed we get a very extensive bright colour range; like the primroses they are good for several seasons.

If by chance either the primroses or the polyanthus are in the way after flowering I lift and replant them close together in a shady spot, then provided they are never short of water they remain fit and well until the autumn, time for the move back to their flowering quarters.

It is difficult to believe that *Pulsatilla vulgaris* was once a wild flower of the meadows, in March our single plant raises a mass of flower heads, each one of exquisite beauty and a month later the seed heads are in great demand for flower arrangements. We have one or two hybrids but none can compare with the one-time weed we treasure here at Clack's Farm.

Some twenty years ago a kind friend gave me a few *Fritillaria imperialis* bulbs (crown imperials); no mistaking them – they really do smell strongly. They were mixed, some yellow ('Lutea maxima') and some coppery red ('Aurora'); they are flowers which are often seen in cottage gardens. They need to be left undisturbed for years, this is what we have done and it has certainly worked. The bulbs have multiplied rapidly whilst flowering has been consistently good, nothing puts them off their stroke more than a garden fork around them. I mark their territory with canes otherwise it is so easy to damage the emerging shoots which sometimes start as early as late January. Weeding around them is a job to be done by hand. We have been successful in harvesting some viable seed and now we wait for about four years to see if we have any hybrids, crosses between the two; I hope so. The only feed we give ours is a top dressing of compost after they die down in June for their six-months' sleep.

Soon after we came to Clack's Farm I discovered a few lilies of the valley roots smothered in weeds. I rescued them and planted them close to a wall where the soil is always damp and never gets a glimpse of the sun. Now after several lifts and divisions they fill the whole border, they love the conditions and repay us for the care and attention with nodding heads of great delicacy with a perfume that is nature's real thing, a scent that has never been equalled.

A plant that has only once failed us is *Helleborus corsicus* when all the stems broke under the weight of snow during the winter 1981/1982, but the roots were truly hardy and the plant survived. For the flower arranger it is a must, its huge clusters of apple green flowers last so long, they are there from March till the end of May and after that the seed heads are just as beautiful. The seeds fall and germinate freely, so much so that on Open Days we are often able to give a few seedlings away as a reminder of what we hope has been a happy day.

April

We have many plants which would please the flower arranger but none of our garden plants is grown specifically for that purpose. Both Riet and I prefer to look at nature's own arrangements, the *Bergenia* is one such plant, its large rounded leaves tinged with red in the winter and spring provides a delightful backing for the cyclamen pink flowers from April onwards. It is a generous plant and does not mind a few of its leaves being removed early in the season; in fact I regard it as useful tidying up. As our flower arranging friends love them the job gets done without our help.

A humble plant collected from a bog *Caltha palustris* (marsh marigold or king cup) is sited close to our small pool. With its buttercup flowers it brings back memories of permanent pastures golden with buttercups and the marshy banks of little streams on the Isle of Mull, yellow with their blooms.

Many frown on aubrieta simply because it is to be found in so many gardens but in April and May it adds a lot of colour to our garden. It is true that its foliage is dull for the rest of the year, but after flowering I trim it back and give the lot an overall spray with malathion to deal with the possible red spider and then, if I remember, a repeat application a fortnight later. There was a time when I planted named varieties but now plants grown from seed ('Carnival' mixed) are so good, with such a good colour range and plenty of vigour, that for mass planting the results have been most successful.

May

By the time May arrives our greenhouses and cold frames are bursting at the seams with all the half-hardy bedding plants in various stages of hardening off before being planted out. Getting plants gradually acclimatized to the tougher outdoor conditions is part of our growing programme. We start planting out early in May, *Dianthus, Verbena,* asters, stocks and such like first; then we come on to the marigolds, petunias, salvias, etc., and finish up in the third week with the geraniums, begonias, etc. The more tender ones may have to wait until the first week in June. This bedding out programme involves raising all our plants from seed, about 15,000 in all including 1,000 F_1 hybrid geraniums. Not everyone would be in favour of bedding out on this scale but it does give us colour throughout the whole summer, without bedding plants our garden would be very dull in August and September, months when we receive a lot of visitors.

The F_1 hybrid geranium seed must be sown early in January. This we do and we are able to have several varieties in bud at planting out time. Growing geraniums from seed eliminates the rust problem so common in the south of England. There are many varieties ideal for treating in this way; my first love was 'Sonnet', a delicate pink flower and its zoned leaves add to its beauty, throughout the season it remains as it started a compact plant. Two others from the same U.K. breeder, 'Cadenza', a rich scarlet and 'Caprice', a coral pink, are both good garden plants. With us 'Red Elite', brilliant red with bright green foliage has been the first to flower but 'Playboy' mixed is the one to go for if you want a more dwarfing variety in a considerable range of colours, it certainly is an excellent choice for a limited area or for patio containers. For an outstanding bright colour show I should mention 'Dianthus Queen of Hearts', a few years ago we had a small group of it no more than 6 × 6 ft (1.8 × 1.8 m) in a border but it stood out above all the rest in an aerial colour photograph of the garden. Another variety called 'Snowfire' has also done extremely well, its white and red flowers will brighten up any garden.

Whilst I never hesitate to try out new varieties, I sometimes have my doubts about the blue sky catalogue descriptions until I have actually grown the flowers myself. Petunias, for instance, are marvellous bedding out subjects, they love the sun and when it shines day after day they are glorious but what a dull lot they can look during a wet period. Thank goodness dwarf 'Resisto Rose' is the exception; it has a total disregard for the weather. We use it liberally and from June to October it has never let us down, it glows with colour all the time. In this context I should also mention the Joy family, which includes several colours, pink, purple, red, rose and white, all terrific flowerers and all have a considerable degree of weather resistance.

Begonias

Begonias are probably our most favoured bedding-out plants, they do well in sunshine but will also thrive in shade. They do much to light up some of our otherwise dark colourless borders. Unlike petunias they are not weather conscious but they do often appreciate a watering as some of our borders shaded by trees can be so dry even in wet weather. I have been delighted with the new series of F_1 hybrids 'Ambra', they are truly remarkable. I have never known fibrous rooted begonias to flower so well. We have been pleased with all the colours, pink, rose, scarlet, salmon, white picotee and white. Mixed seed is also available but I prefer groups of the same colours. Both 'Danica' rose and scarlet make much larger and taller plants but what a show of colour they give us and their shiny bronze foliage adds to their beauty.

I shall never forget growing for the first time 'Non-Stop' begonias from seed, they were F_1 hybrid tuberous rooted plants. Riet potted some on for house plants and they were superb but the few I bedded out stole the show with a flower quality that was staggering. Since that early start before the seed was marketed we have grown the whole range of colours (apricot, bright red, golden orange, pink, rose, salmon, scarlet and yellow) outside. In the autumn we lift the corms and dry them, keeping them safe from frost so we can plant them out again the following season. The seed is certainly expensive but once you get a start you will never need or wish to be without them in either the garden or on the windowsill. They are wonderful – a great credit to the plant breeder who brought them into the gardening world.

I have always been fond of *Impatiens* (busy Lizzie), for years they were pot plants but at Clack's Farm they are not popular indoors as Riet had to wage a continuous battle against the greenfly. However, outdoors, it is a different story, they can be great and will happily flower both in sunshine and shade. For several years we have been searching for the best outdoor variety and have now satisfied ourselves that the F_1 'Futura' hybrids have all the qualities needed. Here again the plant breeder has produced a wide range of colours, all clear and bright from scarlet to white. At first we had difficulty in germinating the seed, now we mix our own compost especially for them without any added fertilizers, it is simply a mix of equal parts of peat and sand. We slightly compact and level the top of the compost, sow the seed without covering and then water before popping the tray into the propagating frame set at a temperature of 65°–70°F (18°–21°C). Like the begonias they do like moisture. Surely they must become more popular; we would not like to have a garden without them now.

I could not omit to mention the portulacas which we loved when we first saw them in New Zealand, they were so bright and cheerful in the sunshine; like the mesembryanthemums without the sun they close up and wait. However, they are still one of my favourites; for instance the F_2 hybrids 'Calypso' planted fairly close together make a floral carpet whilst 'Grandiflora' double with its longer stems and striking bright colours smile at us whenever the sun shines.

There was a time when I was not particularly interested in marigolds, for one thing the smell of the foliage put me off but now I appreciate their bedding out value and qualities. They are so easy to grow from seed, some of the newer introductions flowering within seven weeks from the sowing date. I hasten to add that the names given to some of the new F_1 hybrids, which are interspecific crosses between African and French types, had no influence on my assessment of their botanical qualities! The fact that this new break in plant breeding was achieved in the U.K. aroused my interest and desire to try them out. 'Nell Gwyn' was marketed first, followed by 'Suzie Wong', then came 'Moll Flanders' and soon 'Mata Hari' will be added to the list. At

a

F_1 hybrid marigold 'Moll Flanders'.
(a) In flower eight weeks from seed, ready for planting out in May. The plants were picked out into standard sized seed trays, 28 per tray. (b) Each plant is carefully planted with a trowel, the hole being made large enough to accommodate the root ball without damage.

b

Clack's Farm they have been the first marigolds to flower, they don't need dead heading and go on flowering freely until they are cut down by frost in the autumn. These 'ladies of the evening' are a great acquisition to our bedding out schemes.

Salvias did not do well with us until we started to work in a little NPK fertilizer before planting them out. Now, with extra plant nutrients available at the start, they never fail. Two new varieties have been outstanding, 'Volcano' the earliest to flower and 'Concorde', both are really bright red.

For the antirrhinum enthusiast I must mention the F_1 hybrids 'Coronette', I have never seen larger spikes, nor more closely set florets which stay in good condition for such a long time. If you grow them from seed remember that they like to be on the dry side in the seedling stage.

Summer

By June the colour in the garden increases daily. Our first rose to bloom is 'Pink Perpetue'; we are encouraging two of them to cover part of the south facing wall of the house. 'Pink Perpetue' has proved to be an excellent choice, a good grower, free flowering and with lots of fragrance. At one time we had several island rose beds, then in 1980 we decided to scrap them all as the ground had become a little tired of roses and we decided on a complete new rose garden. We were privileged to have the help of John Mattock in this venture. He prepared the plan and supplied the roses, 44 different varieties, and the planting was completed in March 1981. Now with its background of Larch-Lap fencing and magnificent archway made from oak branches, made by a local craftsman, this new rose garden is another success story.

Every rose in the garden has great qualities; unfortunately it is only possible to comment on a few. I start with 'Robusta', a hedging rose with a growth habit comparable to 'Queen Elizabeth' but even more vigorous, its large bright red single blooms with golden stamens are a dream. Introduced in 1981 it must be popular before long. Then there is 'Matangi', one of the series of 'painted' floribundas from Sam Mc-Gredy, we consider it to be one of the best of that group. 'Trumpeter' is the floribunda that never stops flowering during the season, it just goes on and on producing its glorious large trusses of bright red roses, a real winner. One of Riet's favourites has also found a place, 'Just Joey' with its soft apricot/peach coloured blooms and although the individual flowers do not last long, they are a real visual feast when just half open. 'St Boniface' is another great red floribunda with a small dainty orangey/red flower, near perfect when not quite fully open.

'Snow Carpet' is a pet. Some say it could be used for ground cover which I doubt; however, when it is in full bloom covered in tiny white double roses it lives up to its name, covering the ground with 'snow' in June.

We just could not plant a rose garden without finding a place for 'Albertine'; it must be a great rose to have survived ninety odd years and still be popular in spite of its vicious thorns. Ours now covers the archway exit from the garden, it is trained up one side and down the other, what a show it gives us, surely there is no rose more beautiful or more lavish with its perfume.

John Mattock included 'Rubrifolia' mainly for its foliage and hips, to be used in Riet's flower arrangements. Now in its little corner it pleases us both. Nearby close to the fence are several climbers which we are treating as tall bushes and they are co-operating; an old favourite 'Handel' is there excelling itself for health, vigour and free flowering – it is in a class of its own, an exceedingly beautiful rose.

We have no naturally wet areas in the garden, the one that is a little moist is not far away from the septic tank. It is here that *Meconopsis betonicifolia* (Himalayan poppy) flourishes with its unbelievable blue flowers. Not only does the damp soil there suit it but it enjoys the slight shade all day. We save our own seed and sow it immediately after harvesting, then it germinates like mustard and cress. Store it a few weeks and the germination can be very disappointing. Two things to remember here, first, sow in trays and just leave them standing outside – don't give them any protection even during the coldest winter weather; secondly, both seedlings and established plants die down completely in the early autumn, I mention this as so many good plants have either been thrown away or destroyed, given up for dead because there were no signs of life above ground.

We are fortunate in having a soil that suits lilies, all we have to do is add some good, well-rotted compost before planting them in a slightly shady position. We have grown all our 'Regale' lilies from seed, again sown immediately after the seed is ripe, as with meconopsis we leave the seed trays out in all weathers. From seed they start flowering in their third year but in the fourth year they are really at their best, masses of fragrant, trumpet flowers on plants free from virus. But for more fragrance plus a virus problem we have that old timer *Lilium candidum* (madonna lily); we know that it is a risk to grow it but for me it has treasured memories of friends and cottage gardens. No other lily has beauty and scent to equal it. We try hard to keep it well away from all our other lilies and so far we have succeeded in preventing the spread of the insidious virus disease.

I have a soft spot for 'Enchantment', it flowers on short stems and instead of hanging downwards the open light mahogany/orange blooms look you straight in the face. We have been pleased with the way that 'Pirate', a relatively new variety, has multiplied; it has the same flowering behaviour as 'Enchantment' but a much darker and brighter reddish/mahogany colour. Just one tip, we use small marker canes to tell us exactly where our lilies are resting, a mistake with a hoe in the spring can be fatal to an emerging shoot, it is one of the areas where we weed by hand, a little tedious but safe.

In June our delphiniums are majestic and with so many named varieties we are privileged to be growing some of the best. But one grand show a year is not enough to satisfy us, so once the early summer blooms start to fade we cut them completely down to ground level. After that we give them another feed and if need be a good watering. Within days new growths emerge and go on to produce a second fantastic display in September. Contrary to general belief this practice does not exhaust the plants; we see to that with the extra feed of PBI Back to Nature fertilizer and a light cultivation to work it in.

Autumn

As the days shorten and the autumn sunlight becomes more golden we find the Red Admiral and other colourful butterflies in plenty, taking life easy as they sip nectar from the sedum (stone crop) flowers. No plants can be easier to grow, every little piece of growth is a viable cutting, we have two varieties 'Brilliant' and 'Autumn Joy', both well named.

From early autumn onwards we go indoors and there we have many favourites to brighten up what could otherwise be a dull time of year. So now we leave the garden and come into the house, where we find some seventy or more houseplants.

Houseplants

I have mentioned the pleasure we get from our greenhouse gardening, now here indoors we are able to see some of the fruits of our labours. Each and every downstairs window has a sill laden with pot plants either in full bloom or showing off its attractive foliage for which it is grown. The production of the flowering plants is so planned that when one batch begins to fade another lot is ready to take its place.

This is particularly true in the case of cyclamen, by staggering the sowing dates, starting in early January and finishing early in March, we are always able to have the window sills filled with plants at the peak of their flowering from October till March. As a matter of fact by growing the plants cool in the greenhouse every one of them gives us weeks of glorious colour before tiring, so different from the experience with cyclamen forced by high temperatures into early flowering. All these plants grown from seed form excellent corms during the first year and at the end of the season we dry them off for friends who have not got the facilities for growing from seed; they are able to start them off again in August for another colourful winter show.

We have no difficulty either in germinating the seed or growing the seedlings on. When large enough to handle comfortably the small seedlings are potted into $2\frac{1}{2}$ in (7 cm) pots, but not before that small pot is full of roots are they potted on into larger ones. We always water from the bottom and feed with a liquid fertilizer once a week. We grow several varieties, for the larger flowers and plants our choice is 'Firmament Mixed' (an F_1 hybrid) which gives us a wide range of colours. In addition to the beauty of its blooms 'Decora Type Mixed' has great variety in its well marked silvery foliage. Then for fragrance we have a few 'Sweet Scented Mixed', the flowers are on the small side but in a warm room the perfume is always there. We never grow any of the F_1 hybrids in just one colour, we leave that to the commercial grower. We like variety so for us it is always a packet of mixed seed.

Now that the plant breeders have succeeded in shortening the streptocarpus leaves and getting at the same time larger flowers, the plants do sit more comfortably on our windowsill. The variety 'Bandwagon' mixture has a pleasing range of colours, white, pink, blues and a light maroon, all with beautiful markings in their wide open throats. Once a streptocarpus starts flowering it will go on for about six months, sometimes even longer. 'Prize Strain' is another selection that has done well with us. We have never found it easy to grow streptocarpus from seed; it germinates then the seedlings stand for weeks, the same size, just surviving and waiting for the urge to grow. We have needed a lot of patience, making sure that neither the seedlings or the young plants are ever in the full sun. However, when fully grown and flowering the plants do not mind sunlight.

Amongst our favourite foliage plants is *Iresine herbstii*; it is a plant that asks for little, just water and an occasional feed, but it gives such a lot especially when the sun's rays fall on the wine red leaves. It is a great experience on a sunny winter's day to see such colour in a foliage plant, only nature can provide such a glowing picture. It is easily propagated from cuttings, rooted first in water and then potted on in the usual way; we get nice bushy plants by nipping out the growing point of the rooted cutting when it is potted on.

For variation indoors during the winter we lift from the garden some fibrous rooted begonias and pot them up, for this to be successful it must be done before the first frost but plants specially grown for winter flowering indoors have given us the best results. The most successful one has been Lorraine 'Love Me' an F_1 hybrid. Sown in March/April it will flower from October with a profusion of clear pink flowers until the following March. Another successful variety has been 'Kalinka' (red and rose), it is larger flowered than the Lorraine 'Love Me' – it too will flower right through the winter months.

We have found gloxinias rewarding plants, most of ours are grown from seed sown early in the year. As with cyclamen we are all in favour of mixed colours and recently we have been very impressed with the 'Castle' strain. Again the secret for a long flowering period is never to subject the plants to very high temperatures during the growing season, either in the greenhouse or in the room and to remember that they don't like powerful sunlight.

For several years we have grown *Begonia rex* from seed and have now got some fascinating plants with the colour patterns different in every one of them. From one packet of seed we get all sorts, some are small while others go on to make enormous plants, we are very selective keeping only the very best. All of them do flower and some of the flowers are rather attractive while others are very insignificant but they all contribute to making our rooms cheerful.

Sadly we have had to give up growing primulas, we both love them but Riet is allergic to them, so while others can have the pleasure of their glorious flowers and tending such popular ones as *P. malacoides* and *P. obconica*, our interest is limited to seeing them elsewhere. There are of course many other houseplants I could mention but I have kept in the main to my favourites which we grow from seed.

SIX

Shrubs and climbers

Flowering shrubs make a great contribution to our garden. Once I had completed the initial tree-planting exercise I started to clear and clean the ground in front of them. From experience I knew that to start planting shrubs before the ground was absolutely free of perennial weed roots would be asking for trouble. Even though it took a whole season before every trace of couch grass and ground elder was dead and eliminated, my patience has been rewarded. Shrub borders choked with perennial weeds indicate that the pre-planting jobs were done superficially or that there has been a lot of neglect since.

Ground preparation

I started with weeds and rubbish galore. Picking out every piece of weed root was not on for me doing the job single handed, I dug the lot in with a full sized spade, not my old 'shortie', making sure that every single bit of green growth was below ground. After that I kept a sharp eye open waiting for the next move which came during the next few weeks when the weed growth broke surface. When that happened I was quickly out with my Wolf three-pronged cultivator to break the surface and the clods up, after that I dealt easily with the new weed growth (see p. 115).

My idea was to start clean and I have remembered since to go round thoroughly under the shrubs with the hoe several times each season. I have not yet found a weed resistant to the treatment and what pleases me most is that the Dutch hoe does not disturb the roots nor does it have any adverse effect on the shrubs; in fact it stimulates them. Many of them appreciate a little air in the soil and as a result, with the soil surface broken, they get more benefit from the summer rains.

I always make a point of selecting young plants; large, older shrubs may look much more attractive but it is the young ones with active roots that get away quickly and ultimately make the better and more healthy plants. I still prefer to plant during the dormant season November to March and the earlier during that time the better.

Planting/feeding

Whilst some shrubs and climbers must be pot grown otherwise they do not transplant well, for the rest I prefer to plant with bare roots, as lifted direct from the nursery, I can then make sure that the root ends are neatly trimmed to remove any damage which ensures healthy and quick new root development. For more people, however, container-grown shrubs are now the order of the day, their roots are tightly compressed within the containers, which means that the root pattern is far from normal and it is only after planting out that the shrubs are able to develop naturally below ground. It is during this establishment period that a container-grown shrub needs extra care especially if it is planted out during the growing season, death through the root ball drying out is a common happening.

Whereas some advocate putting rich farmyard manure in the planting hole I start with either nothing or just a handful of sterilized bonemeal, my policy is to wait (as with trees) until a shrub has re-covered from the transplant operation, then when it has made its new roots I decide whether to feed or not. A scattering of well-rotted compost as a top dressing at that time is never wrong, it is natural food, applied when the soil is moist it will prevent drying out. Only when a shrub lacks natural vigour do I resort to fertilizer feeding, then my choice is a liquid feed with a high potash content tomato fertilizer, such as Tomorite. Over feeding a shrub or climber could result in too much leaf growth and no blossom. Whilst it is difficult in a small-sized garden to have some shrub or climber in flower every day of the year, I set out from the beginning to spread their flowering seasons as widely as possible. I was determined that Clack's Farm garden should not be devoid of colour during the winter. So to cheer us up at Christmas time we have quite a number of shrubs in flower but my pride and joy at that time is a mahonia, its racemes of lemon yellow flowers are too erect for it to be a *japonica* so I have come to the conclusion that it is a *bealii* hybrid. All I know definitely is that it came to us as a cutting from a friend and it is a wonderful free flowering plant, so free flower-ing as a matter of fact that its fragrance is overpowering on a mild winter's day. After flowering comes the red leaf colouring and these leaves are in great demand for flower arrangements, so to prevent absolute nakedness I have imposed a ration system. I was planning to plant in 1982 the more erect growing variety *M.* × 'Charity', but now, after the harsh winter of 1981/1982 when it was decimated in our part of the country, I have decided to stick with our *bealii* hybrid, it is hardy and so easy to propagate from cuttings.

Another delightful December to February flowering shrub is *Hama-melis mollis* (Chinese witch hazel), the one we planted 20 years ago is now 8 ft (2.4 m) tall but we hesitate to reduce its height and risk losing even for one season the pleasure of seeing and scenting its clusters of fragrant yellow blossom. In a more open position it would give a bonus of autumn foliage colour but we are content to have it as a herald of a new gardening season.

Winter to spring

From the kitchen window we have a clear view of two of my favourites *Jasminum nudiflorum* (winter jasmine) and *Garrya elliptica*. The jasmine is trained along a stone wall with its narrow branches opened out like a fan, from November to February the entire length of these leafless branches is clothed with lemon yellow golden flowers. The secret of success here is to cut back the long growths immediately flowering has finished and encourage the new growth with a liquid fertilizer feed.

After years of unimpeded growth and magnificent displays of its long greyish catkins each winter we are now nursing our *Garrya* back to its former glory. Coming as it does from California, the recent winter 1981/1982 with its −24°C killed practically every branch but thank goodness its roots survived sufficiently to stimulate some dormant buds into life. After removing all the dead wood we made sure that it had plenty of moisture and a liquid feed to help it on its way.

I have never regarded skimmias as being in any way spectacular plants but I do regard them as being useful as they are all evergreens, slow growers with neat and tidy compact growth habits, they also do well in some of our shadier spots. We have two white varieties and one red one, 'Foreman' and 'Japonica' are both generous in their production of creamy white fragrant groups of flowers which open in April and last until the end of May. 'Rubra' has not only darker foliage but the closed flower heads are cheerful during the dark winter months and a glorious sight when fully open in April. To get the winter bonus of brilliant red berries a male japonica plant is needed to ensure pollination of the flowers produced by female plants, a ratio of one male to three female plants seems to work admirably.

Although forsythias are so common we still have a place for them, my favourite variety is 'Lynwood'; its upright branches are simply laden with rich yellow bloom each spring. We control its size and maintain its flowering vigour by cutting back the old flowering wood immediately the blossom starts to fall.

If I had been writing this chapter prior to the 1981/1982 winter I would be telling you about our several camellias which in years past have been so wonderful each spring. I always appreciated that the flowers were tender, consequently ours were all sited so that in the event of a frost they were shaded from the early morning sun. Alas, in that severe winter all our camellias suffered – it mattered little whether they were varieties of *C. japonica* or *C. williamsii*; all their wood above the snow covering was killed, and some fared worse and were killed totally. All I can say is that we are hopefully replanting again making sure that the soil will be slightly acid and moisture retentive. I am a great believer in peat for camellias, they love it. In my opinion 'Donation' with its large clear pink semi-double flowers must head the list, it has all the qualities needed for the small garden, it is vigorous, erect in growth habit and quickly settles down to regular flowering. Incidentally whenever I have had a camellia reluctant to flower I have found an application of sulphate of potash at the rate of 1 oz per sq yd (34 g per sq m) does the trick.

Magnolia

Magnolias share the camellias' liking for a moisture-retentive soil and here they do well because our soil is also lime free. Our 20 year old *Magnolia* × *soulangiana* and *Magnolia* × *soulangiana* 'Alba Superba' both have complete protection from the cold north winds and from the strong south westerlies; it is this protection afforded by some large old hollies that has enabled them to reach up to well over 12 ft (3.6 m) without damage to either branches or loss of bloom. Both are free flowering; 'Alba superba' comes into flower with its pure white, large, cup-shaped scented blossom just a week or so later than the more common *soulangiana*. Whilst both are protected from the early morning sun 'Alba superba' is free from it for another two hours and this makes quite a difference after a frosty night. It is always a great disappointment when some of the outer petals are singed brown.

M. stellata which flowers a fortnight before *soulangiana* is even more subject to such damage but what a glorious sight it makes in a frost free March and April. Whilst *stellata* is a slow grower I have found *M. liliiflora* 'Nigra' even slower and now after ten years we have a compact plant no more than 4 ft (1.2 m) in height. Its intermittent flowering starts in May and goes on throughout the summer. I love the blooms which stand up like large Darwin tulips, dark purple opening out to reveal a creamy white inside. It will never be a prolific flowerer but it is a plant with great charm, well suited to the small garden.

I have made it a golden rule never to prune a magnolia. On the rare occasion it has been necessary to remove the odd small piece of dead wood but never living wood. Just one tip: a magnolia should always be container grown, don't disturb the roots when you plant it out and don't forget if need be to water it regularly.

April

At one time flowering Japanese quinces were very popular, everyone knew them either as *Cydonia japonica* or simply as japonica; now catalogued as *Chaenomeles* they are either not recognized or forgotten, which is rather sad. At the moment we have only one plant, the variety 'Knap Hill Scarlet' and what a glorious display it puts on each May! As I write I have decided that we must find a place for 'Cardinalis' with its crimson scarlet flowers, 'Moerloesii' a delicate pink and white one, 'Crimson and Gold' with its deep crimson petals and large golden anthers and the last one on my list is 'Rowallane' with large blood-red flowers, the one that did so well with me in Nottingham. All of these are easy to grow either in an open border or in front of a wall, in which case pruning after flowering is a good idea; incidentally our 'Knap Hill Scarlet' is in a semi-shaded position, it obviously loves it and glows with colour each April. Your garden centre will know what you want if you ask for a japonica, stating the variety.

I must not forget our flowering currants which, because we use them in places as screens, are allowed to grow tall without pruning. Grown in this fashion they are most effective and beautiful especially 'Pulborough Scarlet'.

Flowering at about the same time in April is *Spiraea × arguta* (bridal wreath), its long thin arching graceful branches are simply covered with pure white flowers. We prune ours hard back immediately after flowering, this treatment prevents untidiness and ensures prolific flowering each year. The variety 'Anthony Waterer' responds well to the same treatment, not only do we then get a lavish crop of bright crimson flowers but also early in the season some variegated cream and pink foliage. These spiraeas along with many others are easy plants to grow, they give so much in response to just a little care.

Daphnes are short-lived shrubs. Ten years is just about the limit so we do have to work on a replacement basis but this is relatively easy. Seedlings can often be found close to the parent plant, we lift them carefully and pot them up for a period of extra attention before planting them out into their flowering positions. Following this line we are able to enjoy *D. mezereum* and *D. mezereum* 'Alba' to the full, they are such friendly plants flowering when the weather is still cold in February and March. Both are deciduous and completely hardy, their flowers are beautiful and have fragrance. Our other daphne is *odora*, its flowers are even more fragrant but it is not quite as hardy although, with a little surgery afterwards, it survived the 1981/1982 winter.

For our *Pieris* 'Forest Flame' we chose a spot where it has the protection and shade of an old nut tree, there the soil is deep, well

Flower arranger's joy, *Mahonia bealii*, with its older leaves developing autumn tints.

Magnolia x *soulangiana* 'Alba Superba' shielded from the early morning sun, displays its blooms with little or no frost damage.

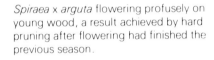

Spiraea x *arguta* flowering profusely on young wood, a result achieved by hard pruning after flowering had finished the previous season.

A small shrub *Cytisus* x *beanii* repays us for planting it in full sun and for trimming it back each season after flowering, by this massed display of flowers.

A young, six-year-old *Acer pseudoplatanus* 'Brilliantissimum', glowing with its spectacular spring foliage; a good choice for the small garden.

drained and is lime free. It has only been with us three years but it is already evident that it likes the conditions and that it is more hardy than we thought. It is a plant we fell in love with when we saw it in Inverewe Gardens on the west coast of Scotland. Now we have the joy of seeing its magic day by day, leaves which change from red through to pink then on to creamy white before finally turning green. In due time we expect it to produce its drooping racemes of lily-of-the-valley like flowers. In the meantime we are more than pleased with its glorious spring foliage colour.

Like most gardeners we have plants associated with memories of people or places, *Lonicera × americana* (honeysuckle) was one such given to me by the late Rowland Smith. Every year it is magnificent, so free flowering and certainly one of the most spectacular perfumed honeysuckles, I shall always be grateful for the gift of that cutting, a beautiful memory of a great gardener.

A little earlier in the season (April) *Amelanchier canadensis* delights us with its fabulous display of white blossom, each and every branch is liberally smothered with flowers. We are able to allow them space so they make even larger shrubs but in smaller gardens they could be pruned after flowering to control their size.

Whilst a spring walk in a rhododendron garden does excite me with its colour and beauty, the dullness of the foliage during the rest of the year is not what we really want in our garden. So our rhododendron growing is now limited to low growing varieties such as 'Elizabeth', 'Blue Tit' and 'Praecox' plus *Rhododendron yakushimanum*, a present from Geoffrey Smith. According to Geoffrey it is a most spectacular plant, its bell-shaped flowers start rose colour in bud then open to apple blossom pink before finally turning white. We have yet to see it flower but the silvery downy young growth has been beautiful. Our azaleas, mostly deciduous varieties especially the 'Exbury' hybrids give us a lot of pleasure; our lime-free soil evidently suits them.

May

But in May it is *Viburnum tomentosum* 'Lanarth' that delights us most, when its spreading branches are covered with large clusters of snow white flowers. They make a wonderful sight against a backcloth of apple green foliage. It is a shrub worthy of a place in any garden and is not fussy about whether it gets the sun or not. At the same time another of my favourites is in flower, *Choisya ternata* (Mexican orange blossom) with its fragrant, star-like, white flowers, in fact this is only its first flush as it does produce some during the whole season. At all times its glossy evergreen foliage is attractive and it is tempting to crush a leaf or two to enjoy the aromatic perfume. It is a shrub for a sheltered position.

Generally weigelas are not exciting shrubs but they have a place in our borders, maybe because they need little attention. However 'Newport Red' with its bright red flowers does make a good show as does 'Bristol Ruby'. *W. florida* 'Foliis Purpureis' with its purple foliage and rose pink flowers together with *W. f.* 'Variegata', both slow growers, have a greater appeal, especially when I see a glint of sunlight on 'Variegata''s golden variegated foliage nursing its rose pink flowers. After flowering we do cut back some of the old flowering branches to give the young growth more space and light.

Cytisus × *beanii* is one of my pet small shrubs. We found a place for it among the rocks in front of the pool, there it loves the sun and the dry situation. During May and early June its wiry, arching branches are smothered with masses of bright yellow flowers, a feast of beauty.

Our lime-free soil is a great advantage, if need be we can add lime; had it been there naturally our shrub list would have been more limited. So here we have no difficulty with *Halesia carolina* (snowdrop tree) which, in spite of its common name, we treat as a shrub but what an unusual one when in May its spreading, still leafless branches are bedecked with silvery white miniature 'snowdrop' like flowers.

June

Then in June, for my birthday, *Kolkwitzia amabilis* (beauty bush) is lavish with its graceful branches bending down with loads of small, foxglove-shaped flowers, pure pink with yellow throats. It is truly my mid-summer favourite, another shrub to prune after flowering.

In June the various *Philadelphus* (mock orange) are also at their best and we love 'Virginal' with its generous gifts of semi-double, pure white, strongly perfumed flowers, 'Belle Etoile' and its exquisitely scented, white flushed, pink flowers and 'Beauclerk' with its larger, sweet scented, white and flushed pink blossoms. At this time the deutzias are also in their full glory, being so easy to grow they should be more popular, 'Montrose' for instance with its large open mauve pink flowers or 'Magician' with its scented, lilac pink tinted flowers. In addition we have *D. scabra* 'Pride of Rochester' a double white tinted pink, all are superb and only need cutting back after flowering.

At the back of the borders we planted some syringas (lilacs), in flower they are beautiful but for the rest of the season uninteresting to look at. We have overcome their ever increasing height at which they blossom by drastic cut backs every few years, then we have to wait a couple of years for flowering to restart. First on my list is 'Mrs.

Edward Harding' with its semi-double scented red flowers, then the popular 'Madame Lemoine' with its large panicles of highly perfumed white flowers and as a third choice the strong upright growing 'Charles Joly' which produces its dark purplish-red, well-scented flowers a little later than most lilacs. Behind the rockery I planted a low growing species *Syringa velutina (palibiniana)*, it is now fully grown and only about 4 ft (1.2 m) tall with nearly the same spread. In May it is covered with erect panicles of fragrant, lavender pink flowers, a real gem suitable for any garden, however small.

At this mid-season time the potentillas are at their best, left to nature the bushes tend to be untidy and leggy, we give ours either a late autumn or early season trim with the shears to make them shapely. We have planted 'Red Ace' so that it is not too badly bleached by the sun, in its shady position the bright red colour is retained. 'Moonlight', another recent addition with flower colouring to match its name, has already proved a success but our old favourites 'Katherine Dykes' and 'Woodbridge Gold' with their primrose yellow blooms are still the dominant ones here.

We have enjoyed the co-operation of the British Fuchsia Society and with their help have a plot of about 20 varieties of hardy and semi-hardy fuchsias. Planted deep it is surprising how well most of them cope with our winters. Whilst we have the established hardy favourites such as 'Mrs. Popple', some of the newly acquired plants have become favourites too. To name but a few, 'Genii' with its golden foliage as well as its spectacular flowers has proved to be a really hardy one, then the more dainty 'Lady Thumb' and 'Son of Thumb' grace the plot after two winters. We were very surprised when 'Annabelle', a so called tender variety, survived the severe winter of 1981/1982. We do make a point of taking several cuttings of each variety we grow outdoors just in case we lose the parent plant during the winter.

Clematis

I must not forget our clematis. Riet's yardstick is 'Jackmanii' with its ability to produce masses of large violet-purple flowers, if any variety flowers as well she declares it satisfactory. I have tried 'Jackmanii Superba' but it lacks vigour in spite of all our extra attention. However, several other large flowered varieties have come up to expectations including 'The President', 'Lady Northcliffe', 'Scartho Gem', 'Walter' and 'Richard Pennel' and several others. 'Barbara Dibbley' is outstanding here, each season it covers its large cane wigwam with a wealth of wine coloured flowers. We also provide a wigwam for our *C. macropetala* (the downy clematis) on which to display its semi-double, nodding flowers of deep lavender blue in April/May; sometimes it decides to give us a short repeat show in the autumn.

We stick to the simple clematis rules, practically no pruning for early flowering varieties, light pruning for those flowering in June but we hard prune the August/September flowerers in early March. An exception to this rule is that rampant grower 'Tangutica', which covers one of the walls in the tea garden; we prune it hard in March. From June onwards its bright yellow lanterns light up the whole wall – it should become as popular as the montanas for this type of situation.

Lower down the order of our summer flowering shrubs are the hydrangeas. Here my favourites are *H. macrophylla* 'Blue Wave' (a lace cap) which stays blue on our soil, none of the pink varieties stays absolutely pink unless we give them a watering with lime water several times during the growing season. On a north wall we have a *Hydrangea petiolaris* which for three years sulked after I planted it and that is normal. However, once it got going it grew rapidly, clinging as it progressed up the clean brick wall; I mention a clean brick wall as it will not cling if the wall is cement painted. Ours evidently loves a north wall and we are always grateful for its overall display of large greenish white florets closely packed together, giving a magnificent show early in June. In August *H. paniculata* 'Grandiflora' never disappoints us, providing it is cut back hard in the spring and what a sight its masses of creamy white flower heads make before fading to pale pink. Another shrub we prune hard each spring is *Caryopteris clandonensis*, this treatment produces the most glorious display of violet blue spikes which starts in August and goes on until October.

By that time *Viburnum tinus* (laurustinus) 'Glyne Castle' planted close by our front door greets us with its pink tinted buds which open to white heads, then it becomes a show of blossom that stays with us until March. *Viburnum × bodnantense* has completely won my affection, it starts flowering in November and goes on until February. A severe frost may blacken the deep pink flower buds or the extremely fragrant rose coloured clusters of open flowers but, with a few days of milder weather, it is back again in all its glory.

There are many other shrubs and climbers I could have mentioned had I been preparing a catalogue. Some people will be surprised that I have not included a mention of dwarf conifers: yes, we planted several 20 years ago, but they are no longer so dwarf. However, they are allowed to stay – had they been favourites of mine some might have been included in the next chapter.

SEVEN

Trees

Having watched our $\frac{3}{4}$ acre ($\frac{1}{4}$ hectare) ornamental garden mature over a period of 27 years it is still difficult to believe that in 1956 it was a derelict pig-run area of the farm, close by the house. The only trees at that time were a few hollies in a hedgerow and some nut trees in the middle. Right at the start we grubbed out the nut trees complete with stumps and roots, it would have been a serious mistake to have left the roots in the ground, it would have been asking for a plague of honey fungus, a disease which can be disastrous, especially for newly planted trees. Whilst the hollies we retained are now large, the prickly leaves shed in April are literally a thorn in our flesh. Thank goodness several of them are females and at Christmas we are always prepared to forgive them, the sight of 20 ft (6 m) high trees covered with glowing red berries is truly heart-warming.

Making a garden from scratch it was tempting to start by clearing a small area near the house in order to get a colour display quickly, however my approach was just the opposite, I decided that tree planting must come first even if it meant clearing circles in the rubbish to do the job. I could wait for roses and bedding plants; trees take years to grow.

Planning

The planning for the tree planting was done indoors by standing at each of the downstairs windows in turn, gradually I built up a mental picture of what the garden might look like in 25 years' time. I decided that trees should form a backcloth for the garden, in other words set the scene but that they should be so planted that no axe or saw would ever be needed. I wanted trees that could and would be allowed to grow to their full natural beauty; nothing makes me more sad than to see a tree beheaded simply because it has grown well, a tree so treated never recovers its natural shape or beauty.

In these garden-centre days it is so easy to take an impulse fancy to a dear little tree in a container and it all too often is a weeping willow which is the most unsuitable tree for a small garden, apart from its ultimate size its quest for drains and desire to block them is unequalled.

The joy of gardening

The time spent at the downstairs windows was well worthwhile as now with alterations to the house and every window sill lowered there is not a tree in a position that restricts the view of the garden. We can, as I had always hoped, sit in a chair and enjoy the garden however bad the weather is outside.

Choosing specimen trees for planting in what was to be a lawn was not easy. I settled for two, one a *Prunus avium* 'Plena' (the double gean cherry) which has made a beautifully shapely round head. Each late April or early May it gives us a glorious show, masses upon masses of long-lasting, double, pure white, pendulous blossoms. To stand under the tree with the blue sky beyond the laden branches is akin to taking a step into heaven. My second choice for the lawn was *Betula pendula* 'Youngii' (Young's weeping birch); it has made a graceful tree with its branches reaching down to the ground, no flowers on this one but it does give us some autumn foliage colour. It is a tree that has a tendency to produce an occasional longer branch but this can easily be removed without harm to the shape of the tree. Neither of these trees impede the long view of the garden from the house.

For a position in what was to be a circular bed I planted *Pyrus salicifolia* 'Pendula' (willow leaved weeping pear). It quickly made a dense amount of weeping branches, the removal of the lead at planting time has meant that it is more compact than our two others planted elsewhere. These latter ones are now tallish graceful trees with weeping branches and they flower profusely in April. This tree I would recommend for a small garden especially as the foliage is silvery grey and makes an excellent contrast to the more usual green.

Flowering cherries
Being an ardent lover of flowering cherries I planted quite a number in the garden plus an avenue of mixed varieties alongside the approach lane and what a joy they are each April and early May. In November/ December to cheer us up it is once again flowering cherry time and what a delight on a dull winter's day to see *Prunus subhirtella* 'Autumnalis' in full bloom. To name a few of my successful, favourite flowering cherries: 'Pandora' in full view from our lounge window, its pale pink flowers brave the cold March winds and always cheer us up; I did not despise the popular 'Kanzan', I like its upright growth habit and its annual display of great clusters of rich pink double blossom is terrific, no wonder it is so popular. 'Shiro-fugen' is another free flowerer, it starts with dainty pink buds before going on to produce masses of double white flowers, it could never be a mistake to plant this one. I selected *Prunus serrulata longipes* with its broad spreading

growth habit for planting close by the entrance gate; its long stemmed pendulous flowers, pale pink in the bud stage which open to double white, make a glorious welcome to all Clack's Farm callers in mid-May.

One of the greatest is 'Tai-haku' (great white cherry) and what a show it makes for our benefit every April–May time, the fact that its masses of snow-white blossom have the contrast of the coppery red foliage compels us to stand underneath its branches and absorb its magical beauty. I must not omit 'Ukon', certainly one of my favourites, its semi-double flowers tinged with ivory, slightly green and its bronze foliage makes a delightful combination. Nor should I forget 'Erecta', an upright grower which was given a position where space for side growth was limited, it has done well but I have been a little disappointed about its flowering ability. Our real disappointment is 'Accolade'; in Nottingham it was wonderful but here the bullfinches only leave us with blossom at the extreme tips of the branches so we have never seen it in its full beauty when early in April it should be covered with its dainty pink blossom.

If you plant flowering cherries do what I did, scatter a little garden lime around the planting hole and some bonemeal in the hole and do not forget to stake and tie the trees, they will need support for several years. Another point: be patient as it will be about three years after planting before they start to take off.

Flowering crab apple trees
In contrast flowering crabs settle down to grow almost immediately and several of ours are now quite large trees. Each April–May we look forward to their magnificent display of colour and have never been disappointed. In addition a few of them are very attractive in the autumn, *Malus* 'Golden Hornet' for instance has masses of small bright yellow fruits which when seen in the autumn light give a show of sheer unadulterated beauty. By the way it does an excellent job in the spring as a pollinator for several of our ordinary apple trees. The ever popular *M.* 'John Downie' also has its place, but for the finest flavoured crab apple jelly we have three Siberian crabs which I propagated from an old tree in Lord Trent's Lenton House garden.

Our two very large Wisley crabs are very popular with wine making friends and we are more than pleased for them to collect the often too large crop of purplish red apples. When ripe they are certainly very colourful but inedible and jelly made from them has virtually no flavour. However, according to several friends, they make a good rosy-pink wine. For a great spring flower display I planted *M.* × *eleyi*, another one of my favourites; I love its deep wine red blossom and the purple hues of its foliage. *M.* 'Profusion' is another one that has been outstanding with its masses of red to purple, flushed with darker red, flowers which turn to purplish pink before fading, it too produces small fruits oxblood red in colour.

I have always wanted a horse chestnut tree (*Aesculus*) but to have planted one in the garden would have been folly; its place was in an open field and now after a quarter of a century it stands majestically with its spreading branches – each May its candles of blooms are a glorious sight. In the garden, however, there is space for a red horse chestnut, *Aesculus × carnea* 'Briotii', a smaller tree but still not a subject for a small garden. Where there is space and patience to wait for it to blossom it can be very rewarding, after 20 years ours now flowers freely each May.

Tulip tree

I do have some patience but after 25 years I am still waiting for our *Liriodendron tulipifera* (tulip tree) to flower. I planted it hopefully after seeing a superb one in Oslo in full bloom. At the present time the tree is fully 20 ft (6 m) tall, I love its large almost square leaves but would like to see a few flowers in my lifetime, even if they have to be at the top of the tree.

Strange as it may seem after writing the above paragraph I walked out into the garden bathed in July sunshine to discover to my amazement three fully open blooms and several more flower buds on the lower branches. So for the first time I was able to look closely at the tulip tree flowers. It was not difficult to understand why it has acquired its common name but few tulips can have such a delightful combination of colours in their petals, all subdued, ranging from light green, orange through to pink – in just a magic moment my patience was more than rewarded.

Maples

I have always been fond of maples (*Acer*) but however large the garden and surrounding area there can never be room for more than a few. *Acer pseudoplatanus* 'Brilliantissimum' which makes a smallish tree is delightful in the spring, its large buds unfold first into shrimp pink then to pale bronze and finally green leaves, a colour transformation which I find exciting – a must for a small garden. Our other maples, *A. plantanoides* 'Drummondii' and *A. p.* 'Goldsworth Purple' were planted alongside the drive. Here their contrasting foliages are most effective, 'Drummondii' with its green leaves margined with cream and 'Goldsworth Purple' clothed with its dark red purple foliage.

The winter of 1981/1982 with its −24°C frost at Clack's Farm ended the lives of our *Eucalyptus gunnii* and *Cupressus macrocarpa* 'Lutea', the latter a 20 year old specimen and far taller at 30 ft (9 m) than suggested in many catalogues. A *Cedrus deodora* which had grown up during the last 25 years into a perfect specimen tree we viewed each morning from the kitchen window, now alas is also dead. It is fortunate that all our other trees did withstand the extreme temperatures. A lesson was learnt for the future – we shall take more note of the native habitat before planting a tree; we can have and do have severe winters at Clack's Farm from time to time.

Conifers

Our most beautiful conifer is *Cedrus atlantica* 'Glauca', again it is a tree that needs space, not only for itself but so that it can be seen at a distance for its graceful beauty to be fully appreciated. Right from the start I took care to plant conifers as single specimens as it is so easy to finish up with a garden looking more like a dull cemetery than the bright and cheerful garden it should be and which I aimed at.

We have a *Sequoia sempervirens* (Californian redwood) which came to us as a seed on a Christmas card from San Francisco some 20 years ago, now it is at least 30 ft (9 m) tall and dwarfing everything around it. In the U.S. a specimen reached a record height of 366 ft (111 m), even in the U.K. they can reach well over 130 ft (40 m). I just wonder now whether I planted ours in the right place, they have been known to live 2000 years growing taller all the time but that's not my worry!

Sorbus

Coming back to the deciduous trees, I must mention *Sorbus* 'Embley' (*S. discolor*), a mountain ash with just the right upright growth habit for its position. It lost no time in establishing itself, it has never put a branch wrong nor does it ever fail to come up with a long lasting show of glorious bright red shades of autumn colour. I must also note two varieties of the common whitebeam: *Sorbus aria* 'Majestica' (*S. a.* 'Decaineana') is a great favourite in the spring as is also *Sorbus aria* 'Lutescens' when the upper surfaces of its leaves are covered with a dense creamy white down.

Robinia pseudoacacia 'Frisia' is another tree which we both admire in the spring when its yellow foliage greets us and remains colourful until the autumn when it turns coppery before leaf fall.

Whilst many despise laburnums some simply because they are so common, I love 'Vossii' with its long racemes of golden flowers; this one is true to the common name golden rain tree. It is unfortunate that the seeds are poisonous and a risk to children but 'Vossii' produces much less seed pods than most.

There is certainly not enough space in this book to mention all our trees but I must include *Populus candicans* 'Aurora'. Although it is not suitable for smaller gardens, we have used it to screen a 60 ft (18 m) long Dutch barn with great success. Its young shoots are bright pink sometimes streaked with red and yellow, followed by deep green mature leaves speckled with many creamy silvery colours. This is one of the few trees which gives more colour when it is cut back annually than when it is allowed to grow normally. Thus it is not spoiled by a periodic cut back, a treatment which might possibly contain it in a more limited area but like all poplars it is a hungry feeder and its roots do wander great distances. Whatever you do, don't plant it near the house or close to any drains.

The loss of some forty elm trees on the farm is gradually being put right not only by growing some oak seedlings but also by the planting of a few beech which do well on our soil; in addition we have chosen *Platanus acerifolia* (London plane) for its relatively rapid growth habit. For the oaks, we collected a quantity of acorns during an autumn visit to Apeldoorn in Holland, some from a tall red specimen. The young oaks are already looking good, nearly four feet tall after only four years from seed, so it could be said that we are still planning and planting for future generations.

We have also planted a group of three *Betula pendula* 'Dalecarlica' (Swedish birch) within sight of our back door; already after only three years their bark is gleaming white. Here is a tree with a narrow head and delightful feathery foliage that can be planted in a not too large garden.

Just a final word about planting trees: make the hole large enough so that you are able to spread the roots out. I never put rich compost or farmyard manure in the hole, I wait until the newly planted tree has got over the shock of the transplant before thinking of giving it a feed. The only treatment our trees get at planting time is some bonemeal to encourage re-rooting. Newly planted or transplanted trees regularly need watering especially if the weather turns dry and that extra care will be advisable until they become established in their new home.

EIGHT

My methods of weed, disease and pest control

Clack's Farm is no exception to the rule, we have always had our fair share of pests and diseases. However, we like to think that it is anticipation and prompt action that prevents any serious damage.

Weeds

As regards weeds, we started with the worst of the bunch, couch grass, ground elder, docks, thistles, bindweed, to name but a few. In the cultivated areas we conquered these with the Dutch hoe, now visitors see our weed-free borders and find this difficult to believe. It is our contention that any weed denied the opportunity of producing above-ground growth dies within six months from exhaustion – without foliage growth the roots are unable to replenish vital food supplies so death within a short time is certain. This approach to weed control only works if the hoeing is a regular operation and the ground is kept absolutely clean, a single lapse resulting in above-ground growth and you are certainly back to square one. We have not used weedkillers to this day on the cultivated areas but we do find Tumbleweed invaluable for keeping some of our out-of-the-way 'rough' areas free of weeds.

For years we have been on top of the perennial weed problem but surrounded as we are by land not all that clean, farmland annual weed seeds do drift in, in considerable quantities. Here again it is the cultivation methods that succeed; wherever possible we turn the soil over before Christmas, then in March we start the routine spring cultivations. First it is a round with a Wolf three-pronged cultivator to break down the clods (this upsets any overwintering weeds), then come April when the soil begins to warm up and weed seed germination starts, it's a second round with the cultivator which deals death to weed seedlings whilst they are still in the white thread stage – that's the round that wins more than half the weed control battle.

From then on we keep the Dutch hoe on the go, remembering all the time that one year's seeding means seven years' weeding. We get very disgusted with ourselves if we ever have to use a wheelbarrow to carry the weeds away, it just should not happen. Take my advice; do not expect your compost heap to get hot enough to kill weed seeds, the theory is all right but it does not happen in practice.

Diseases
It is anticipation that enables us to prevent serious outbreaks of disease.

Black spot
Take for instance black spot on roses; we start by spraying with Murphy's liquid copper fungicide after pruning in November and repeating the application in late February, that is about the time when the spores are released from the dead diseased leaves and enter the scales of the swelling buds. Systemic fungicides may have some effect during the growing season but once the buds are infected black spots will in due time appear on the mature foliage. This does not mean that systemic fungicides are of no value, so much depends on the life cycle of each individual disease. We now rely entirely on Boots systemic fungicide for the control of powdery mildews and have found it excellent on roses; without it our delphiniums would be ruined long before the second flush of spikes in the autumn.

Apple and pear scab
The Worcestershire climate favours such diseases as apple and pear scab, their spore release occurs when the weather is warm and humid. Here again it must be prevention as there is no cure. Infections result in large, blackish, unsightly patches on the fruit. For years we started off with captan at the bud-burst stage, it was effective and safe on all varieties but now we have switched over to Boots systemic fungicide as this controls apple mildew at the same time; captan on the other hand seemed to encourage mildew. On the apples and pears we repeat the spray at fortnightly intervals avoiding the open blossom stage, not because the fungicide is dangerous to the bees but we add insecticides to the spray to control pests at the same time.

Pests
We are certainly not short of fruit pests but Murphy's Lindex added to each fungicide spray application takes care of both the sucking insects (aphids, etc.) and the leaf-eating caterpillars. Fruit tree red spider is not a serious pest with us but just in case we do add malathion insecticide to the post-blossom application.

On strawberries aphids would be a pest and certainly increase the risk of virus diseases spreading and for this reason we add malathion to a systemic fungicide spray just before blossom time. The fungicide has done much to reduce mildew and grey mould on the berries at fruit picking time.

Raspberry beetle

Raspberry beetle, the pest responsible for maggots in berries, used to be a problem until we sprayed towards the end of the blossom time with PBI Back to Nature insect spray. Here again it is a job we do in the late evening in order not to harm the bees and other pollinating insects. We have found this somewhat old fashioned insecticide based on rotenone (the active ingredient of derris) and quassia, most useful against many sucking and leaf-eating insects. We like the product as it is of vegetable origin and therefore safe. Incidentally it has on occasions solved different pest problems on house plants (including some in the greenhouse), where the greenfly and whitefly had become resistant to the more potent organo-phosphorus insecticides. Applied once a week PBI Back to Nature insect spray has done a wonderful job.

Aphids

We are very fond of our beech hedges but the first trim in the spring can be a very sticky business due to beech aphids which, if allowed a free hand, can build up and breed at an alarming rate. We deal with it soon after the young leaves unfold using a systemic insecticide based on dimethoate which is absorbed by the leaves and remains active for about three weeks. The same insecticide enables us to control greenfly whenever it turns up in the ornamental garden, it is excellent on roses too. When we have need to spray shrubs, trees and some of our longer hedgerows we use a Bio-hoser at the end of a hose pipe, this cuts down the time needed and we can reach trees far beyond the bounds of a hand sprayer.

Whilst we are always careful to use insecticides, fungicides and weedkillers according to the manufacturers' directions, our choice is always directed towards those known to be safe, especially when they are used in the vegetable garden.

Vegetable pests

Vegetable pests are widespread in our district; without action cabbage rootfly, carrot fly and onion fly would cause havoc. The cabbage rootfly lays its eggs close to the stems of newly planted brassicas; it adores cauliflowers more than any of the others. During the past two seasons we have used Secto insecticide-impregnated brassica collars and have had 100% control but these collars only work when they are put in position immediately after planting and the plants are free from eggs or maggots at that time. For both carrot and onion fly we have been completely successful by sprinkling Bromophos granules in the open drill at sowing time and following that up with a watering of a

Murphy's Lindex solution about a fortnight after the seedlings have emerged.

For caterpillar control on all our brassicas we use PBI Back to Nature insect spray, it is safe and effective. We watch for the first appearance of the cabbage white butterflies, then we are out with the sprayer before the caterpillars hatch out or have a chance to do any damage. By the way we have tried many different types of sprayers, some better and less exhausting than others but since switching over to the Wolf re-chargeable, battery-operated sprayer the job has become so much easier and less tiring − it is now a job that does not get put off till tomorrow. The battery is kept at the ready fully charged.

Perhaps I should mention potato blight, the disease that does sometimes turn up here in August or September especially if the weather turns warm and muggy. At first a few brown patches appear on the foliage, in a bad outbreak the potato tops are totally killed and the spores are soon washed down to the tubers. It is often suggested that the disease can be controlled either by pre-disease fungicidal applications or by applications at the commencement of an outbreak. I have little faith in either and have found it wiser to cut off the haulms at the onset of the disease, burn them and wait for the potato skins to firm up before lifting for storing. The alternative approach, even if effective, means that the spores go into the ground and so on to the tubers; this results in many of the potatoes going rotten later on in store.

I have left slugs and snails until last; they are no longer a problem at Clack's Farm although we did start with masses of them. My obsession to keep weeds down to a minimum, to have no untidy corners full of rubbish, has paid off, coupled with our regular annual digging. The secret of slug control is to deny them breeding ground and living quarters, they adore dirty damp corners. Winter digging exposes their eggs which become food for robins etc. and it is well to remember that too much rich farm manure or compost can increase the slug problem especially on clay soils.

A last word about soil insects: it is not necessary to know the name of every one. A general rule is those that move quickly are friends, they feed on other insects; it is the slow movers that do the damage to the plants, when you find them destroy them, don't wait to name them or have them named.

Index

Index